THE PREACHER

JUSTIN THORNTON

Love you Sis,

I pray for you and Brian,
and I thank God ya'll are in
my life. I hope this helps you
love ; spread the Gospel,

DEDICATION

This book is for my favorite people on God's green earth. Anne, Anabelle, J.D., and Selah, you are my world and I cannot believe God let me be your Father and Husband.

This book is for my parents and my sister, who showed me how to follow Jesus.

This book is for the countless people who have poured into me. I can only hope to do the same for others. This book is an effort toward that.

CONTENTS

FOREWORD

Foreword by Drs. Ron and Wanda Walborn

One of our greatest joys working with college and seminary students for over 30 years has been watching young men and young women develop into leaders and people of Kingdom impact. Our dear friend and former student, Justin Thornton, is such a man who has grown into a strong leader, brilliant communicator and strategic thinker. This book on preaching the Word of God is timely and much needed. In many ways, the student became the teacher. As we read through these pages, we both found ourselves saying things like: "That's really good!", "I never thought of that!" And even an occasional "AMEN!"

The older we get, the more we realize there is so much we don't yet know about the Lord. We do know that the Word of God reveals the ways of God and leads us to the will of God. As the Apostle Paul said, even on our best days we still "see through a glass dimly." Even though Jesus is the same yesterday, today and forever, our perspectives change and our understanding of God and His Word changes as we grow and experience Him in deeper ways.

We all love the facts, certainty and answers, but we also must learn to live in the glorious mystery of a God who has revealed Himself through His Word but will never be fully known this side of eternity. It means we must trust the Holy Spirit to continue to illumine Scripture in His God-breathing way. We must resist the temptation to box our understanding and experiences into a formulaic approach of how He will act. The Word is faithful and true, but it is also living, active and sharp, cutting off parts of us that need to be pruned and exposing places in our hearts and minds that are much broader and deeper than we were willing or ready to handle at the time of our first reading or study of a text. That said, the Word of God will not return void and it will accomplish the purpose for which it was sent—that is good news for any preacher!

Standing before people to preach the Word of God is a frightening, sobering, exciting gift all rolled into one. It is unlike teaching in that it takes a small portion of Scripture and immediately calls the church, both individually and corporately to knowledge, faith and action. A preacher receives the burden of the people to carefully study the timeless truths of Scripture to catch the background, context, attitude and message of the ancient author and communicate that to the 21ˢᵗ century audience. It takes work, practice and repetition to learn the art of delivering a sermon, but it takes just as much work, practice and repetition to faithfully study and "live" through a text personally before talking about it.

In *The Preacher—A Comprehensive Guide from Heart to Pulpit*, Justin Thornton does a great job explaining all the parts that go into the craft of preparing your own heart first, then embracing the process and delivery of the Word. When Justin took our Homiletics class at Nyack College, it was stressed that sermons needed to have three important qualities. First, they needed *clarity*. "If the trumpet does not sound a clear call who will get ready for battle?" (1 Cor. 14:9). In essence, we trained young preachers to tell people why they needed to hear this message, say it clearly, then call the hearers to a specific response based on that truth.

Second, every good sermon must have the quality of *relevance*. How many sermons have we sat through that just don't scratch us where we itch? A good preacher prepares sermons with eyes on the Word, one ear turned toward heaven and one ear turned toward the needs and cries of the audience. The Word of God is always relevant if we discern the time and context correctly. Finally, we taught our young preachers to expect the Word of God proclaimed to have an *impact* on everyone listening. Preach for response. Preach for the will. Preach for repentance. Preach for renewal. You may not always give an "altar call," but expect the Word to have an impact on your listeners. We would often pray the words of Jeremiah over these men and women as they prepared to preach in class or in chapel, "May His words be like a fire in your mouth and his people the wood it consumes." Being willing to stand before a group of people to preach the word week in and week out is a courageous endeavor. It goes with the territory of pastoring others, but few people make the time in their schedule to steward this gift well and hone it as a skill to be developed. Justin Thornton does both very well. His life is a godly example of one who makes time and space for the Lord to move His heart first, then prepare that Word for others to grow in their relationship with the Lord. In this book, Justin helps the reader find his or her own voice while at the same time being true and faithful to the inspired truth of the Word of God. Well done, Justin. Thank you for this gift.

PART 1 THE PREACHER'S HEART

CHAPTER 1

RESTORING THE VALUE OF PREACHING

It was the first time in my life I was going to speak in front of people where the moment carried weight. I'm not counting the regrettable high school speech class presentation— a moment riddled with puberty and fear. I was in Puerto Rico on a mission trip with a group from my college. I had recently been promoted to team leader because the other leaders had forgotten that they were Caucasian and next to the equator. While they nursed their sunburn wounds in an empty church, I was trying to figure out how to be a leader. I was terribly selfish and filled with pride. Even though I became the de facto leader due to weather conditions and neglect, somehow it all went straight to my head.

This was an evangelistic trip where we would go into some of the toughest parts of Puerto Rico and perform an interpretive dance about Jesus on the cross and then someone would share their testimony. This may sound like a nightmare, but it actually had great impact, drawing attention and questions from eager listeners. We took turns giving our testimony. My turn was on a hot Thursday night in a place called *El Horno*. It translates "the oven" and it was not just known for its heat, but for its drug activity and poverty.

On the drive there, I had a Jacob-like wrestle with God… except I did not win, and he did not name a nation after me. I was whining to him about everyone on my team. I was complaining about how hot it was and how chicken and rice was on the menu for every meal.

I was less like Jacob and more like Jonah as I whined about my "first world" issues. I was consumed with myself, and I was supposed to get up in front of people and talk about Jesus.

I stepped out of the van and as my feet hit the pavement, my selfishness hit a wall. I looked around and became keenly and spiritually aware of my surroundings. In that moment, I was given the heart of God and I saw the pain of the people around me. Puerto Rico is a beautiful territory full of beautiful people with an amazing culture. The Christian community there is vibrant, passionate and capable. But, just like every other place in the world, Puerto Rico has neighborhoods in need of restoration and redemption. This specific neighborhood was broken, and that brokenness confronted all my spiritual senses. Selfishness was overwhelmed by selflessness. Pride lost a fight to humility. I had eyes to see and ears to hear, and those eyes and ears were overwhelmed with compassion.

We set up our mini sound system in the middle of their community and began the skit. The person who would be sharing their testimony was always waiting close by for the conclusion of the skit so they could seamlessly step into a speaking role. As I waited for the skit to be over, I experienced a filling of the Holy Spirit. I was shaking, not from fear, but from burden. I was ready to preach because God called me to this moment. I don't remember the content of the message, but I remember proclaiming passionately the gospel of Jesus Christ and the grace He poured over my life. With tears in my eyes and power on my tongue, I called the people to respond to Jesus. And they did just that. Many gave their life to Christ that night, but one gentleman will always stick out in my mind. He was walking on the fringes of the neighborhood under the influence of a specific drug cocktail unique to that area of Puerto Rico. In his account, the Spirit of God stopped him so violently in his tracks that the lollipop in his mouth fell out. His heart became open to the message of Christ, and he asked one of our leaders to pray for him. I don't know what happened to that man, but on that night there was a look on his face of genuine surrender.

This is the power of the proclamation of the Gospel of Jesus. A moment where Jesus takes an imperfect but willing vessel and uses them to bring light into the darkest nooks of humanity. This is a moment where lives are changed, and surrender is secured. A moment where real repentance is but a vomited confession away. This moment is robust and holy and has the capacity to bring an entire people back to God. The Scriptures, both Old and New Testaments, chronicle moments like this one, where generations are shifted, and new cities are built on new foundations. And yet, this moment— a moment of Spirit-filled proclamation— has been devalued. This moment has been traded and bartered for other practices that the Church thinks more critical. It has been sold for rhymes, tweetable phrases and shallow lists. There has to be some curiosity about the shift. Why did preaching, which is clearly of high value in the Scriptures, become so devalued in recent decades?

Preaching Devalued—The Should

Why have we devalued preaching? I think the first reason is a diverted obsession that we can call *Micro and Missional Attention. Micro and Missional Attention is when we spend all our currency of attention on Micro and Missional endeavors, leaving no currency of attention for other faithful endeavors.* We have a vigor to turn the attention of the Church toward these ideas and philosophies. In this effort, we take a "one or the other" approach. It is either preaching or being missional. We tend to focus on one or the other at any given time. It is either a Micro Church model or preaching. Instead of incorporating preaching to compliment both movements, we have forced preaching to take a timeout until we are sure we have given enough attention to micro and missional movements.

Let's start with the precision focus on being *missional.* The word "missional" is used more at ministry conferences than protein powder is used at Planet Fitness. There have been hundreds of books and thousands of churches all hovering around the axis of being missional. The missional movement is a good one, and at its core, is a catalyzing force that helps the church embody the idea of being *sent.* Alan Hirsch, one of the leading thinkers of the missional movement, defines the word missional as our "posture toward the world". A good definition begging the Church to not just face inward anymore. Dr. Elias Medeiros at Reformed Theological Seminary states, "It means to live, think, write as a sent one for the sake of God's glory."[1] The emphasis of being a "sent one" is a sentiment and definition shared by many. For our purposes, our working definition of missional will be, "living as a sent missionary in job, neighborhood and culture".

It has been my personal conviction throughout pastoral ministry to empower, equip and send every believer into their personal mission's field. I read books, go to conferences, labor to live it out in my own life, and preach countless sermons on the topic. It is a faithful endeavor and should garner great attention from the Church. However, I think we should be intentional and considerate about the relationship between preaching and being missional. Attention on one should not mean avoidance of the other.

I have three kids, and our family currently lives in an 1100 square feet apartment overlooking New York City from an amazing place called Jersey City. This apartment, in this location, is a huge blessing and I praise God for it. However, it can be a bit tight for a family of five. This can be especially true during the evening, when all five of us are home. With homework tears streaming, snack crumbs flying, and argumentation abounding, the Thornton household can only be described as chaos. I wouldn't even dare to call it controlled chaos. There is no control. And the fight in this chaos is for attention. "Dad, look at this craft I made." "Mom, can I have chocolate milk, a different pair of socks, a pencil and a puppy in the next 30 seconds?" Okay, that may be a bit of an exaggeration but somehow, multiple questions are piled into a short snippet of time. This beautiful and maddening chaos has caused me to establish a personal rule: "No phone when I get home from work." I have noticed that when I get home from a long day of ministry and my kids and my wife need my focus, the last thing I need to give my time to is a

---

[1] Medeiros, Elias, Ph.D. What Does it Mean to be Missional, *RTS.edu*, Reformed Theological Seminary, Published November 8 2017. rts.edu/resources/wisdom-wednesday-with-dr-elias-medeiros/.

sports feed on my phone. I suppose others may have a greater capacity for multitasking, but I am incapable of doing both. I cannot give my family the attention they need if I'm paying attention to my phone. Attention is currency, and careful stewardship is required. Therefore, I have made a clear decision about where I will distribute my attention. I have decided I need to sacrifice one thing for another.

Attention is certainly a currency in ministry. When your team is working on your vision, mission, core values and the like, you are also determining where your attention will go. In vision-building, much of the American Church has made a clear decision about the distribution of attention, and they don't give too much attention to preaching. We think if we give too much time to preaching, our missional activity will diminish. We think the centrality of what we are "about" will be lost. We think our vision will leak out onto the floor. Because of this fear, we have decided that preaching needs to be the casualty. We will spend all of our attention to mission or other pastoral duties, so that our preaching preparation drops from 8-20 hours down to 2-4 hours. Maybe we can label it the Holy Spirit and just get up there and wing it. Maybe we will become the dreaded Saturday preacher. The preacher who does all of his or her prep on Saturday. Trust me, your congregants want you to know something: the only thing scrambled together on Saturday should be eggs.

Your ministry platform can, at times, feel like five people in an 1100 square feet apartment. I get that just as much as the next preacher. This is why the book *Simple Church*[2] was such a revelation. Every pastor interviewed for Rainer and Geiger's revolutionary text realized that being at the church every day of the week for knitting classes and meatball cook-offs was actually detrimental to the vision of the church. When pastors were called to give attention to the things that were mission essential, casualties were inevitable. Attention to what really matters will make excessive programs fall

Simple Church: Returning to God's Process for Making Disciples. B&H Publishing Group, Nashville, TN, first edition 2011.

like soup cans in the backyard BB gun shooting range. Again, attention is valuable currency that should be handled with great stewardship. Furthermore, preaching should be the last thing that loses your focus and attention.

Preaching is your platform for vision. Preaching is the place where you rally the troops to charge the hill. Not only that, but preaching is also where you tell the troops the location of the hill and your methodology for charging it. It is where you communicate your heart to be missional and what a *sent one* can look like. If you consider your local church an incarnational church, it is where you proclaim the incarnational One and then crawl into the practicum of being incarnational. If your church lives and dies on the heartbeat of justice and mercy, it is where you walk verse-by-verse through everything Jesus said about justice and mercy. Whether you like it or not, God designed preaching as one of the primary ways to communicate the mind, plan, and vision of God. It is biblically and practically undeniable. We must not divert our attention away from preaching, because preaching is how we proclaim where our attention should be in the first place. It is the springboard. It is the pre-game speech. It is the halftime speech. Since attention is currency, my claim is that we don't need to sacrifice missional attention to preach well. We need to value preaching because it is often the mechanism God uses to anchor our people in missional tendencies.

The same goes for our *Micro Attention*[3]. I love the idea of Micro Church[4] movements[5]. The focus to stay small and organic, stay away from big, attractional overheads, and get back to the simplicity of the early Church is something I can't wait to see the Church in the

---

[3] Micro Attention is the precise focus on a micro expression of church. This precise attention can be consuming to the point of ignoring other faithful endeavors.

[4] Micro Churches are intentionally small expressions of the Church that make the elements of the early church and discipleship a priority.

[5] Sanders, Brian. *Microchurches: A Smaller Way,* © Brian Sanders, Tampa, FL, 2019.

West shift toward. The decentralization and shift of focus off a personality toward the empowering of the priesthood of all believers is a beautiful focus. That focus would have complimentary power and substance if we taught our leaders and those with an apostolic view to preach and teach. It does not make sense to abandon the vehicle of preaching the Bible. That would be short sighted, and it would not keep in view that, although the apostles in the early Church were often in smaller environments, they kept the "Apostles' teaching" as a deep value. In the famous list of Acts 2:42-47, the "apostles teaching" was something, not everything. It had its place and time. They didn't lead up to it with a large building, four songs and a bumper video. But it had a significant place in the life of the early church. In other words, let's not swing the pendulum too far as we figure out where to focus our attention.

The modern Western Church has a notorious tendency to swing pendulums. When we swing, it is a violent swing, and the momentum typically takes us too far. Most of the Church realized that, if all our resources and vision hover around the axis of a Sunday morning attractional program, we will not make disciples. I heard Tim Keller define idolatry in a sermon as, "Taking a good thing and making it an ultimate thing"[6]. In the past, the Church in the West may have done that with preaching. Preaching is not meant to be the ultimate thing. It is meant to be the mirror that reflects and projects the ultimate thing. In the realization that Sunday morning became too much of a sacred cow and preaching had become the end goal, we started to do what we typically do, swing the pendulum hard. Instead of placing the art of preaching in the correct category, the category of a really good thing, we devalued it. Now it sits a few pegs below where it should. The momentum of the pendulum took it too far in the other direction.

The second reason I think we have devalued preaching is the *work*

---

[6] Tim Keller, *The Grand Demythologizer: The Gospel and Idolatry.* The Gospel Coalition, Mar 24, 2014, www.youtube.com/watch?v=hN9GyHKrpPI.

and the weight of preaching. Let's start with the work. Preaching is not just hard work; it is unique work. Every Monday, I sit down and turn on some instrumental worship music to block out the noise of the coffee shop. I have a mandate in my gut. Some of it is healthy expectation and some of it isn't. I love the mandate, but I dread it at the same time. The mandate states: "Come up with something original, yet every word should be anchored in the Scriptures. Come up with something inspired and authentic. What you come up with must also be compelling and engaging. It must be culturally relevant to now and contextually relevant to ancient Palestine. It must have story and pinpoint application. It must have good rhythm and outstanding clarity. It must be better than last week and at least a little funny. You must start with prayer, then do the work of exegesis, hermeneutics, homiletics and finish up the week with a really good internalization process. Because the reality is, on Sunday morning, you are going to stand up in front of an eclectic mixture of dozens, hundreds, or thousands of people and it will be just you, the Bible, a microphone and God." This is the work, and I can't think of anything in the world like it. A schoolteacher has an equally hard assignment and is just as underpaid but has a different set of rules throughout the day. There is participation, curriculum, homework and testing. There is permission for dialogue to accompany the monologue. A vocational speaker or a stand-up comedian has a similar pressure and loneliness on stage attached to their job, but they internalize one manuscript and then they are done. They may tweak a joke or hone an introduction, but they will never have the unique challenge of internalizing something brand new every week. The work of partnering with the Holy Spirit and birthing something new early in the week and then owning it so deeply that you have it mostly memorized by the end of the week is tailor fitted to preaching. Preaching is hard and unique work.

I always chuckle a little on the outside and cry a little on the inside when someone says, "You preachers only work on Sunday." I get that statement or question often from people who don't understand the inner clockwork of ministry. It is somewhat shocking that someone would think you can stand up in front of a group of people and rattle off coherent and biblically sound thought. It is certainly not offensive; it just lacks understanding of how hard constructing a good sermon can be. I am not comparing it to a large portion of the labor force out there who break their backs weekly; that also would lack understanding. I am saying that preaching is hard work because it is like having an annoying administrative assistant that pops their head in your office every 10 minutes and reminds you that you still have more work to do. "You still have to exegete the text today. You still have to open that commentary and finish your outline. You still have to memorize the content of your sermon today."

But if the work is like an annoying administrative assistant, then the burden is like a meathead gym instructor. That annoying guy at the gym who keeps putting more plates on the bar, making what you are lifting heavier and heavier, yelling at you with dissatisfaction and Gatorade breath. You know that it is good for you in the end, but at what cost in the present?

Paul talks about this burden as he writes to Timothy and counsels him on what his elder team should look like. *"Let the elders who rule well be considered worthy of double honor, especially those who labor in preaching and teaching"* (1 Timothy 5:17, ESV). It is interesting that Paul uses the Greek word *Kopiao*. It translates, "to grow weary, tired, exhausted (with toil or burdens or grief)"[7]. Paul is speaking of his own burden. Not only does Paul work hard, but he experiences a burden that brings eye-sagging weariness and soul-crushing grief. He goes further, and quotes Deuteronomy: *"For the Scripture says, 'You shall not muzzle an ox when it treads out the grain,' and, 'The laborer deserves his wages'"* (1 Timothy 5:18, ESV). I believe Paul is not just building a case for ministry workers to get paid, but he is also speaking to the burden of preachers and leaders. The ox does not just have work before him, but he has a burden on top of him. He is forever carrying a heavy weight that is attached so deeply it latches onto identity.

---

[7] Blue Letter Bible Institute, *Blueletterbible.org,* Strong's G2872. © Blue letter Bible, 2021, https://www.blueletterbible.org/lexicon/g2872/esv/mgnt/0-1/.

When the preacher stands up, he or she first has the weight of people's burdens. The preacher has been with his congregation, listened to their problems and sometimes, whether they choose to or not, preachers take that burden upon themselves. Now on their shoulders there could be sickness, marital hardship or financial strain. A quick theological jab would be that Jesus' burden is light, and it is not the preacher's job to carry those burdens. And while it is true that we need to cast our anxieties on Him, we are not a wall, and burdens do not just bounce off us like a tennis ball. Additionally, there is theological balance, as God tells us to *"bear one another's burdens, and so fulfill the law of Christ"* (Galatians 6:2, ESV). The preacher also bears the burdens of building and budget. They are haunted by the growth of the church and overarching spiritual themes affecting the church like lukewarm spirituality, poor understanding of the gifts of the Spirit, division and apathy. The preacher walks to the platform carrying a backpack filled with the burdens of the body of Christ.

The preacher bears the burden of opinion as well. Opinion can be the heaviest weight transferring from people onto the preacher. Before each sermon, I pray against the temptation to preach for popular opinion. I pray against my human nature that desires to sanitize the truth to balance the opinions of the few people that I know will send a Monday morning email. This is a burden that we should not carry into the pulpit with us, for it only hinders our power, boldness and anointing. It makes us preach out of fear and anxiety. The Church will always have annoying and opinionated gossip mongers. It is an impotent sermon that is preached for those few lurking in the crowd. This is a truth we all know, but we still carry this burden with us.

The preacher carries the burden of the text as well. Every week, when the preacher studies the text, both hands are filled. One hand is filled with grace, the other hand filled with truth. Yes, that grace is good and light, but sometimes that truth is heavy and convicting. That grace is rescuing and feels like a catapult, but that truth moves like a swift knife in the hands of a brilliant chef. There is so much going on inside of a good preacher that the outside product could never fully explain the inside sanctification. The truth is, the more that the text burdens the preacher, the better the sermon typically is. The more repentance there is and the more times the preacher takes cover under a shelter of grace, the better. That grace usually pours out in emotion, passion and authenticity.

The preacher walks up on stage looking like a parent of five children walking through an airport. There is baggage everywhere, including under their eyes. The burden, the weight and the work of preaching makes some preachers give up. It can be one of the major causes of burnout. The argument may be that there are many causes of burnout, but I would contend that if a preacher didn't have to lug his or her baggage up there every Sunday and vomit out something compelling, there would be much less fatigue and pressure.

The real question is, how does this weight and this work make us devalue preaching? The answer is simple; it is the way we cope. Devaluing preaching is our defense mechanism. It is how we deal with the pressure, the work and the competition. More importantly, it is how we deal with comparison.

I am not well versed in international ministry, but if I am speaking of the American heart, we are competitive. We want to win. We want to be good at something or we quit. Instead of facing up to a truth that we are not one of the best preachers in the land, or our preaching is not reaching everyone that comes in the door, we devalue this thing we struggle with. It is a simple American formula that we came up with all on our own. When we are not good at something, we devalue it. Value higher that which you are good at. We learn it in adolescence when someone is better at football. We tell them, "I am going to take my ball and go home". I think for many preachers, it is much easier to devalue preaching than to do the work. It is much easier to make excuses than it is to deal with the burden. Preaching, however, needs to be of primary value in your ministry.

Preaching Valued—The Why

Every great movement in the world and throughout the history of Christianity has had a great communicator or preacher leading it. If you would, take a moment with me to think through the great movements that you respect and admire. The first person you think of is likely a great communicator who leads or led the movement. Now this is probably the moment where you try and think of an exception to this rule. No doubt, given enough time, you will be able to think of a successful movement that puts very little value on gathering for worship and preaching. Please understand, I am for any movement chasing after the Kingdom of God. But even if you can think of a movement where the leader is not a great communicator, you will still find, at the very least, a good communicator who teaches and casts vision well. The Salvation Army had William Booth. The Christian and Missionary Alliance had A.B. Simpson and A.W. Tozer. Foursquare had founder Aimee Semple McPherson. A reporter said this about McPherson, *"Never did I hear such language from a human being. Without one moment's intermission, she would talk from an hour to an hour and a half, holding her audience spellbound."*[8]. The Methodists had Francis Asbury who is said to have traveled over 300,000 miles preaching approximately 16,500 sermons. Biographer Ezra Tipple said, *"Under the rush of his [Asbury's] utterance, people sprang to their feet as if summoned to the judgment bar of God."*[9]. It is also said that there were only 600 Methodists in America when Asbury began preaching. At the end of his labor, when they had to carry him from stage to carriage because he pushed his

---

[8] Christianity Today, Aimee Semple McPherson Foursquare Phenomenon, *Christianitytoday.com*, Carol Stream, IL, 2021, www.christianitytoday.com/history/people/denominationalfounders/aimee-semple-mcpherson.html.
[9] Christianity Today, Francis Asbury Methodist on Horseback, *Christianitytoday.com*, Carol Stream, IL, 2021, www.christianitytoday.com/history/people/denominationalfounders/francis-asbury.html.

preaching so hard for so long, there were over 200,000 Methodists.

You cannot think of the Great Awakening without thinking of George Whitfield, John Wesley and Jonathan Edwards. As you follow history up to and through the Great Awakening, you can even draw a line to a single sermon. Jonathan Edwards' "Sinners in the Hands of an Angry God"[10] still reverberates hundreds of years later. These revival sermons were stones in the water that would ripple for decades into the future.

Let us examine a little more of the modern era, then circle back to the Scriptures. If you sit in a room full of Baby Boomers and ask them to raise their hand if they gave their life to Christ at a Billy Graham Crusade, I am willing to bet that at least one hand will fly into the air. Whether or not you think evangelistic crusades are a good discipleship model is not really the question. The reality is, God used those events to draw hundreds of thousands of people to Himself.

Great movements are led by great communicators. One of my favorite preachers and men, Martin Luther King Jr., led the undeniably powerful Civil Rights Movement. Other great justice and mercy movements include A21, led by one of my favorite female preachers, Christine Caine. The Southern Baptists International Mission Board was led by David Platt for a time. A great church planting movement, Acts 29, is led by Matt Chandler, and the 3DM discipleship movement has Mike Breen. Our great worship movements have good communicators as well. Hillsong has Brian Houston and Bethel has Bill Johnson. Some of our big city movements include Tim Keller in New York City and Eric Mason in Philadelphia.

But what people have done and how culture has moved is not the

---

[10] Edwards, Jonathan and Smolinski, Reiner (Editor). Sinners in the hands of an angry God. A Sermon preached at Enfield, July 8th, 1741. Electronic texts in American Studies. 54. digitalcommons.unl.edu/etas/54/.

real litmus test for whether something is good. The ultimate measurement of good is what God has said about that thing. When testing a trend or a movement, I want to know what God thinks of it. I want to know if the genesis of that truth is God. I want to know if it is in Genesis. So, let us start there.

From the Beginning

There was nothingness before God spoke. Before God stepped into the pulpit to begin Creation's first sermonic movement, there was emptiness and void. The Spirit of God was hovering over the face of the waters. Then comes the preacher.

"And God said, 'Let there be light,' and there was light. And God saw that the light was good. And God separated the light from the darkness. God called the light Day, and the darkness he called Night. And there was evening and there was morning, the first day." (Genesis 1:3-5, ESV).

Notice that God does not only preach light into existence, but He also names it. He brings application and explanation to light. In Genesis 1, *"God said"* appears ten more times as he creates and names all of creation. He will bless and bring value with his words by calling creation *"good"*. If you think about it, God could have created in any way he dreamed up. God is clearly creative; He is THE Creator after all. And although, as evidenced throughout Scriptures like Jeremiah 32:17 and Isaiah 48:13, God does use more than His voice, He is clearly making a point here about speech. He preached the world into existence.

In that very moment, words and proclamation would become the most powerful tool and weapon this world would ever know. Words can start a war, but they can also end one. Words can bring hell or healing. Who doesn't love this proverb? *"Death and life are in the power of the tongue, and those who love it will eat its fruits"* (Proverbs 18:21, ESV). And if that doesn't grab you, James gets pretty dramatic:

"For every kind of beast and bird, of reptile and sea creature, can be tamed and has been tamed by mankind, but no human being can tame the tongue. It is a restless evil, full of deadly poison. With it we bless our Lord and Father, and

14

with it we curse people who are made in the likeness of God. From the same mouth come blessing and cursing" (James 3:7-10a).

The power of preaching has its origins in Creation and then continues all throughout the Scriptures. God preached truth to His Creation and then His Creation bears God's image and preaches the truth proclaimed to them.

God sends a stuttering Moses to preach to a venom-spewing Pharaoh. He sends Samuel to Saul and Nathan to David. He sends Ezra and Nehemiah to the diaspora of Jews to rebuild their city. Both Ezra and Nehemiah were good communicators, but all they needed to do was to spend an entire day reading the Scriptures word for word. Then all the people wept and turned their hearts to God. They needed only to proclaim the words proclaimed to them.

How can we forget the work of notable prophets like Elijah, Isaiah, and Ezekiel? Men who not only proclaimed the word of God and prophesied from the heart of God, but also suffered greatly for their faithful preaching. God chose them and used their preaching and proclamation to communicate His plan, His heart, and His commands to His people. After hearing from the Lord, Isaiah preached about the birthplace and tribe of Jesus. He proclaimed Jesus' family line and character.

From the very beginning, God's plan was preaching, God's plan was proclamation. Petty arguments can be made that this is Old Testament theology and methodology. But John came preaching the same simple message that every prophet from small to big, from Jonah to Isaiah, was sent to preach. "*Repent, for the kingdom of heaven is at hand*" (Matthew 3:2, ESV). In John the Baptist, God chose to prepare the way for His Son through a messenger, a preacher. In the same way that God had endless choices for how He was going to create, He had endless choices for how He would prepare the way for the Messiah. He chose preaching. Jesus was preaching before puberty. Jesus, early in Luke, quotes the prophet Isaiah and tells us one of the major reasons for His anointing.

"The Spirit of the Lord is upon me, because He has anointed me to proclaim *good news to the poor. He has sent me to* proclaim *liberty to the captives and recovering of sight to the blind, to set at liberty those who are oppressed"* (Luke 4:18, ESV).

Among Jesus' major objectives for the incarnation is the objective to preach (see Mark 1:38). He would do just that, from the Sermon on the Mount to the sermon on the plain to the cleansing of the temple one thing was clear: Jesus was a preacher!

As His disciples followed from an intimate distance, they would learn how to become preachers. They would learn how to speak with the boldness of God in the face of persecution and how to proclaim mercy in the face of pain. They were preachers-in-training as they followed Jesus.

After their training, He would tell His disciples, *"But you will receive power when the Holy Spirit has come upon you, and you will be my witnesses in Jerusalem and in all Judea and Samaria, and to the end of the earth"* (Acts 1:8, ESV). The disciples have to be spinning at this point. Not only did the resurrection just happen and they are still most likely trying to get a grip on this idea, but Jesus is going to leave again. Jesus' plan is to give them a personhood of God, a member of the Trinity, to live in them and to breathe through them. The Holy Spirit will empower them to be Jesus' witnesses—to preach and proclaim who He is and what He has done. A line to obedience would run through the word witness and they would spend the next few chapters trying to comprehend that they are now the conduits through which the world will understand the greatest revelation in all of eternity.

Well, you know what happens next. The disciples get impatient and ignore Jesus' command to wait. They draw straws and elect Matthias to be their twelfth because they need a round number and someone to blame because Judas isn't around. And then something really amazing happens; the Holy Spirit comes upon them like tongues of fire. They all start speaking in different languages. Some of those who hear and witness this miraculous event are confused or think that the disciples are drunk. But we know, as we look on thousands of years later, that the Holy Spirit is submitting a redemptive miracle. The Tower of Babel in Genesis 11 is a picture of the fall and division of mankind. Languages are divided and the people are scattered. Here in Acts 2, the nations come together by the power of the Spirit and the Spirit unifies through language. Then we get our eyes on verse 14, *"But Peter, standing with the eleven, lifted up his voice and addressed them: 'Men of Judea and all who dwell in Jerusalem, let this be known to you, and give ear to my words'"* (Acts 2:14, ESV). Peter preaches.

Peter's sermon is a biblically accurate and precise account of the gospel from old covenant to new, and it is the first sermon in the greatest movement to ever live and breathe: Christianity. Thousands would turn their hearts over to a loving God, and nothing would be the same. A city and a people were forever changed by one sermon. But just like so many other times in the Biblical story, this is not the end of the story of preaching. It is yet another chapter. The apostles' teaching makes the golden list of Acts 2. They carried their deep love for teaching and preaching the Gospel to town squares and law chambers. They proclaimed the word of God and the story of God both when their lives were on the line and in peaceful Bible studies. They made the proclamation of the Scriptures a priority to both small crowds and big crowds. They preached to people with rocks in their hands; they preached to angry mobs. Preaching was the propeller of the Church because it contains the words, presence and power of God.

Preaching was, is, and will forever be, a core value of God's mission. Preaching is ingrained in God's nature. It is a primary color on His palette. The violent collision of His Spirit with an obedient man or woman of God will always be something that has the potential to change lives and even cities. We would be hard pressed to find any conduit used more often in the word of God than preaching to communicate God's heart for people. The late great John Stott said, *"I am an unrepentant believer in the power of preaching."* And:

"There is something unique about preaching. When you have a living person facing living people, hopefully a Spirit-filled, preacher-facing, Spirit-filled people, there is a chemistry. There is something that happens that doesn't happen on television or other forms of communication." [11]

What would happen if we restored the value of preaching? What if we resolved to get better at it? What if every time we stood up to preach the Word of God, we were pregnant with belief that this could be the moment God is healing the people we stand with? We must restore the value of preaching.

The Law of Value

You produce what you value. That is the law of value. I put time, energy and unction into that which I value. I put off, avoid, or cut corners on that which I do not value. I would also say that value is not an unlimited resource. Not only do we produce what we value but we have limited value capacity. Throughout my day or my week, I'm going to invest—my time, my energy, my finance—into the things I value. If you think about it, you can easily tell what a person values by taking a snapshot of their daily schedule or by taking a peek at their bank account. You can tell if they value their marriage and their kids. You can also tell if they overvalue their job and hobbies. You can even tell if they overvalue people's opinions by how much time they spend checking the "likes" on their social media pages. The law of value produces truth.

Every week, my phone sends me a report on how much time I have spent on my phone. To me, it is typically a depressing and sobering reality of misplaced values. After viewing this report, I usually come to the conclusion that things need to change… and then they typically don't. Nonetheless, it is a progress report on what I value.

---

[11] Langham Partnership. "John Stott's Advice for Preachers." YouTube, YouTube, Sept. 14, 2016. www.youtube.com/watch?v=1Q9DtlP8dGw.

I have rules about how I distribute my value capacity. I tell husbands and fathers all the time, "If you want to be a good husband and father, you are allowed 3 sports teams in 3 different seasons." This has always been my rule as a fan. I decided a long time ago, I cannot value an NFL team and a College Football team. That would be poor value deposit. This rule means that my very limited resource of time on the weekends will not be spent in front of the TV both Saturday and Sunday afternoon. My family will notice fast what I value most.

Here is why I bring up the law of value. I think many pastors have poor value deposit. We do not value preaching enough, and therefore we do not dump enough time, energy and unction into our preaching. When we devalue preaching, our values don't line up with God's values. As we have seen, God values preaching. He makes deposit after deposit through a man or woman carrying His torch through preaching. This section is about the heart of a preacher. The heart of a preacher puts great value in preaching. He or she does not devalue it during their week, and it shows in the preacher's schedule. It also shows as God's people gather and the microphone turns on. In that moment, there is great opportunity as the Spirit of God collides with a person of God over the Word of God. That opportunity is not wasted but it is gripped, and according to the Scriptures, the possibilities are endless.

Discussion and Practice

1. Have you devalued preaching, and does it show in your ministry schedule? Why?

_____

_____

_____

_____

_____

_____

_____

_____

2. What do you believe would happen if millions of preachers faithful to the Scriptures and faithful to clarity were raised up?

_____

_____

_____

_____

_____

_____

_____

_____

3. What are two preaching goals that you want to accomplish by the end of this book?

i._____

_____

_____

_____

_____

_____

_____

_____

ii._____

_____
_____
_____
_____
_____
_____

4. Is there something you need to empower someone else to do in your ministry schedule so that you can dedicate more time to your preaching?

What I will stop (empower someone else)

_____
_____
_____
_____
_____
_____
_____
_____

CHAPTER 2

THE HEART OF A PREACHER

Cultivating the Heart

I am *that* guy. The neighbor that you are really annoyed with. The neighbor who is obsessed with his landscaping… I didn't really care until I lived in the suburbs (in my early ministry days) next to a few retired people who seemed to manicure their lawn on a daily basis. Their lawn transitioned into mine and I am about as competitive as the late, great Kobe Bryant. The problem is that it is socially acceptable to have a "mamba mentality" when you play in the NBA. It is not when you are playing monopoly with your kid, trying to shave two minutes off your GPS or trying to outduel your neighbors in a lawn care competition they never agreed to. During this do or die struggle, I did what any competitive person would do. I had someone disciple me in the ways of landscaping. My friend Billy, also retired, would come over a few times a week and teach me the ways of a master-landscaper. To the unsuspecting observer, it must have looked like we were in a movie montage before an international landscaping competition. I learned about what seed to use and when. I learned the peak times to water your lawn and I learned how to stand at the edge of your driveway after a long day of hard work with a cup of sweet tea and two ice cubes, surveying your kingdom with pride.

The primary lesson I learned in all of my training? Priority and attention are directed below the surface, not above it. You must spend time cultivating the soil before you can enjoy what it produces above the surface. Equally, I learned that if you flip your priorities, you will be sorely disappointed in what is produced.

There is a reason that this book is broken up into three sections with this part in first place. As a preacher, what you cultivate below the surface will always be more important than what you produce above it on Sunday. Preaching is first about the heart, then about the technique. This is the way the kingdom of God works. Character always trumps gifting. Isn't this what Jesus is reiterating in Luke 6:45? *"The good person out of the good treasure of the heart produces good, and the evil person out of evil treasure produces evil; for it is out of the abundance of the heart that the mouth speaks"* (ESV). You will produce what you cultivate. To cultivate means to prepare the soil for sowing. The preacher who is cultivating the meditations and soil of the heart will always sow God's favor and anointing. This does not mean his or her gifting will be at peak level as if it is some sort of works-based righteousness competition where the winner gets to be the best preacher. The narrative of the Bible is that we serve a God of the heart first, and so the motive should never be to force goodness for the sake of better gifting. The motivation should always be a child-like devotion to the Father. This deepens the relationship from which God's favor and care flow.

I understand that there are tricks here. Some men and women are good at faking who they are for 45 minutes. They deliver carefully crafted words for, maybe, thousands of people, yet below the surface the soil is cracked and dry. This is like producing a really good-looking weed. It sprouts up fast and it is deceptively pretty. Upon closer inspection, we come to understand that those preachers are producing a good talk, not an anointed sermon. They are peak level performers whose inner life is in turmoil, and that inner turmoil will eventually be exposed.

Preaching is, and always will be, an outer declaration of the preacher's inner life. As such, it is imperative that the preacher cultivates four essential characteristics: authenticity, ownership, brokenness, and meekness. Before these characteristics can make their way into your preaching, they first must make their way into your heart. And they only take root as we pray for them, reach for them and, through great effort, cultivate them.

Cultivating Authenticity

Authenticity is one of those over-used buzz words that continues to come up in the church so often it makes you tune it out and turn it off like an overplayed pop song. However, this pop song earned the right to be overplayed, and is worth at least one more listen.

I grew up in upstate New York in a city called Binghamton—shout out to the 607. There is not a whole lot to love about the broken-down industrial cities of upstate New York. The weather is dark, gloomy and cold, and the career possibilities tend to match the weather. But just like any hometown, you find love in the intricacies of that town. One of the things I love about Binghamton is that people don't talk behind your back, they talk to your face. My circle of friends was not for everyone. They could make Dwayne "The Rock" Johnson cry. But I always knew how they felt. I knew when they were broken, and I knew when they were angry. People often say about me and my friends growing up, "What you see is what you get." I am also a product of a household led by a father who is a Christian counselor. He fostered a culture in the home of honesty in love. When Anne joined our family dinners, coming from a Filipino family without the same face-to-face honesty, she had a hard time stomaching how honest we were all the time. All. The. Time.

I carried that into my preaching. Some pastors cautioned me against openly or freely talking about, for example, lust or my struggles in ministry. I decided, however, to take cues from the people I was ministering to. There was a constant in my research and the main mechanisms for finding that constant were the presence of God and the feedback of the congregation.

By feedback, I am not talking about those broad-brush sweeping encouragements you get after a sermon. I am talking about the encouragements that give measurable feedback that works its way into the testimony of an individual. The constant was that the authenticity of my walk and struggle unlocked courage in others to push past the layers of fake religion that lined their heart like an onion. They had visibility of their sin and they had permission to press into a saving Jesus and a loving Father. My real human struggle led to grace, and that grace was a catapult to sanctification in the hearts, minds, and lives of those who listened and engaged with the sermon.

If you live an authentic, honest and repentant life with Jesus in private during the week, you have an obligation to let that power out in the pulpit. What will pour out of you, in life and in the pulpit, is the grace you feel deeply or your struggle to rest in that grace. Either way, it will produce the presence of God and breathe courage into your people. They will think, "If my pastor wrestles and then has the guts to open their mouth and be honest about it, so can I." It also begins to tear off some of the layers of fake holiness that you have been wearing all these years. Your preaching and inner life will experience freedom, and a preacher who is honest and free is much more powerful than one who is restrained and closed off.

But preacher, be careful. You cannot manufacture authenticity. If your life with Jesus during the week is right off the religious conveyor belt, everyone will notice. People tend to sniff out authenticity, or the lack thereof, pretty easily. A simple mannerism or an eye-brow raise can give away the truth. Standing up in front of people is like standing in the mirror at a department store in the changing room. Truths about who you are, are revealed and sobering. Even those preachers who seem to lie about who they are really well for really long will eventually be exposed. This is not meant to force you either to live in fear of your sin or to overshare. This is meant to implore you to share who you are with discernment. If you are broken, share some of that brokenness. If you are struggling with sin, share how the gospel will rescue you. Let your raw relationship with Jesus be exposed for your people. Of course, I need to make a caveat here. The manner and measure in which you share must have a heaping spoon of discernment. I encourage you to have seasoned leaders around you who share a conviction to be authentic, but also understand the vulnerable nature of the pulpit. Have at least one leader you can trust and run significant "share or not share" questions by.

Cultivating Ownership

The preacher pregnant with ownership is a preacher who produces trust. Trust is an invaluable commodity in communication. Unfortunately, we have years of leaders abusing trust and we have a large hill to climb. It is a hill that can be climbed only one way, owning what you preach. How can you birth a culture of trust? You have to own the truth you are preaching. This engenders trust. Rented or borrowed information just won't do.

I was recently in a notorious fast-food restaurant, and I was deeply ashamed. I was ashamed because I had been doing so well in the areas of diet and exercise, and because I had read some articles about what is in their food and how they make it. However, my feelings were massaged as I watched three members of this particular microwaving establishment sit down and eat their own food. That made me think, "If they know intimately their ingredients and what they are making and they still chose to eat here for lunch, maybe I can ruin just one meal for myself." Their ownership immediately led to a fraction of trust for me.

People will be able to tell if what you are teaching is something you live out and feel. They can test for themselves your emotion and reaction to the Scripture. James is abrasive in his description of people who don't own the faith they talk about: "*You believe that God is one; you do well. Even the demons believe—and shudder! Do you want to be shown, you foolish person, that faith apart from works is useless?*" (James 2:19-20, ESV). Not only will you have a hard time building a trust base with your audience, but also you will be unfaithful according to the Scriptures.

I once had someone I was really close to who was a bit of an anomaly to me. They were a preacher like me, and I would look at their manuscript as we helped each other along in our preaching journey. I thought to myself, "Wow, they have great homiletic technique, and a great grasp on application and illustration." But when they got up to preach, I felt empty and annoyed. I slowly came to the conclusion that the people around me felt the same thing—they sensed the disconnection just as I did. I couldn't quite understand it until I made the connection. This person was not taking ownership of the truth of the text. They were renting the words, but they did not own the life behind the words. They were leasing the ideas on a short contract, and everyone knew it. It came off as one big lie. You can lie about how your life matches the Scriptures for only so long.

Cultivating Brokenness

The Gospel is a story about a God who turns unfathomable sympathy into incarnational empathy. He loves His people so deeply that He decides to become hated, spit on, cast aside, persecuted and crucified. This act of love does bring salvation, as His death conquers sin, and His resurrection conquers the grave. But it also sets the tone for those who are broken and longing to be put back together. People connect with your brokenness. They connect with your struggle with sin, life and ministry. They connect with how far short you have fallen, and how hard you hit the pavement. We need to cancel out the culture of masks. There have been far too many decades of preachers floating up to the platform with their false holiness, never talking about their sin and struggle. They open their mouth and it is riddled with a pharisaic tone and someone who has it all figured out. When the preacher lacks ownership—when the preacher is not honest about their sin, no one goes home with the courage or motivation to face their own mess. Inauthentic preaching fails to give hope. Inauthentic preaching fails to draw strength from the Gospel. People go home to live in shame and performance.

Back to the honest feedback I have received over the years. No one has ever come up to me and said, "Wow, Pastor, your transition from fallen condition to big idea really tickled my soul." They have, however, approached me in tears. and shared with me how my courage to be broken released their confession and ability to not be ok. After all, one of the main sermons from the Scriptures will always be how a loving God meets the broken, not how a loving God consoles the counterfeit. We could certainly make the argument that Jesus' most wrathful comments in the New Testament are aimed at those unable to approach brokenness.

There is a balance here, isn't there? Again, I am not asking you to be the TMI (too much information) preacher. I am not inviting you to overshare in public or idolize your rawness. I am simply saying, as you discern through the Holy Spirit what your brokenness looks like, know with confidence that your brokenness shared in the right moment will bring people to the feet of Jesus, and He can take it from there. Additionally, it will give you accessibility as a leader. People will feel like they can approach you because you haven't been sprayed with holy anointing oil and you haven't been carried into the pulpit in a fiery chariot with Elijah as your Uber driver. The heart of a preacher is one that owns and reveals brokenness.

Cultivating Meekness

Regrettably, meekness is often confused with weakness. Maybe it's because the two words rhyme? Maybe it's because meekness is really difficult to define and translate? Does being meek mean that you are a glorified doormat? Does it mean that your strength is under control? Does it mean that a person has the ability to remain quiet and composed under pressure?

Let's look at the description of meekness found in Jesus' ironically entitled Triumphal Entry into Jerusalem. *"Tell ye the daughter of Zion, Behold, thy King cometh unto thee, Meek, and riding upon an ass, And upon a colt the foal of an ass"* (Matthew 21:5, ASV). Each translation of the Bible takes a stab at the Greek word, some using lowly, some using humble and a bunch using gentle. Even the Bible translators struggle to bottle up this word. It seems to be an emphatic meeting of gentleness and strength. The strength to know when to be gentle. The gentleness to understand when to apply strength. As I look at it in context, I can't help but throw a dart myself. I translate the word as *a humble fortitude with discernment.*

In the instance in Matthew 21, all of Jerusalem is looking at Jesus, and this is His moment. This entrance would rival any HBO special, any awards show and any highly anticipated movie release. Thousands of people gather in the holy city in anticipation to get a glimpse of this man who heals the blind and puts their annoying religious leaders in their place. This is His moment to shine. But Jesus is…meek. He chooses a metaphorical and prophetic entrance that would prove that emphatic meeting of gentleness and strength. His entrance is a concoction of humility and reign. The way He measures out His humility and His perfectly timed strength is something to be worshipped.

The heart of a preacher is one of humble fortitude with

discernment. There is a deep humility and well-directed confidence all at the same time. It is a hard balance to strike and a confusing line to find. I think we should look at it this way. The preacher is humbled when thinking about his or her ability but confident when thinking about God's ability and plan.

I am humbled when I think about the *person*. There is no reason I should be standing up in front of people giving direction of life and dissection of Scripture. Who am I that God would trot me up there? At the very same time, that is the genius of the *plan* of the Gospel. God targeting and showering grace on those who don't deserve to taste that grace. He does it in all 66 books of the Bible. This is the genius of Romans 5:6, *"For while we were still weak, at the right time, Christ died for the ungodly"* (ESV). He didn't wait till we deserved the good news of Jesus. His plan was to choose those who didn't earn anything. Therefore, I can powerfully walk in that plan.

I will often have a young man call me up on a Friday or Saturday to confess sin. They wonder if their unrighteousness has disqualified them from preaching that week. Do they have the right to handle God's word? The innate flaw in that argument with self is that it was never their righteousness that earned them the ability to preach in the first place. I ask them to confess and help them repent, and I tell them to preach with confidence in their Savior the next day. Our confidence is in Him and His plan. It is His plan to speak to His people and change lives. It is His plan that His Word is alive and active and sharp. It is His plan that the Holy Spirit moves through a man or a woman and God's presence sweeps through the midst of His hungry people. It was His plan that He would die for us at the perfect time when we could never earn our right-standing or the honor to speak His word. I have a tremendous humility in the person who preaches, but a holy confidence in God's plan for the word proclaimed. This enables me to enter the pulpit absent of fear and absent of a desire to please human ears. It takes the focus off self or ability, and firmly places it on the ability of the Holy Spirit and the plan of God. Yes, I am unworthy. Yes, I am a sinner. Yes, He has called those with that very resume to preach the good news. He has called me to treat that moment with a true humility and a powerful fortitude. This is my calling, and I won't let Satan poison my mind with fake humility or entice me to cover my face with the mask of religion. I will step into the pulpit and deliver this sermon with confidence in God's plan.

If we spend our time cultivating these postures of the heart, they will show up on Sunday morning. Better than that, they will show up in your process toward knowing the Father more deeply. I challenge you to focus on what is below the surface before you enter part two of this book. There is great tragedy in religious performance, and it is a great source of grief and confrontation for Jesus all throughout the New Testament. Make the crawling journey to the cross and bring all of your baggage with you. That way, you will be sure which way to go when your people need directions.

Discussion and Practice

1. What in your history, upbringing or Church background is keeping you from being more authentic and vulnerable in the pulpit?

_____

_____

_____

_____

_____

_____

_____

_____

2. What can change about your prayer life leading up to preaching a message that will lead you to cultivate ownership?

_____

_____

_____

_____

_____

_____

_____

3. Can you name the masks that you have worn in the pulpit that have shielded the people from your brokenness, authenticity and vulnerability?

_____

_____

_____

_____

_____

_____

4. Do you struggle with pride or false humility? How does that show up in the process of preaching? What does God say about you and preaching that can bring you to a place of meekness?

_____

_____

_____

_____

_____

_____

_____

PART 2 THE PREACHER'S PROCESS

CHAPTER 3
THE VALUE OF PROCESS

God values process and order. He is a God who meets Moses in the desert, out of a burning bush, with a grand mission, but only after he has been formed for decades in a quiet land. He is a God who forms people in prison cells when they never deserved to be there. He is the God of giant fish and land-bound arks. He is the God who created this beautiful complexity in six days and rested on the seventh. In the formed leader, you can see the process God valued and the landmarks He used. In Creation, you see His love for order and its implications. You just have to reflect on the process of photosynthesis for a short time to be in awe of His careful tendencies. You only need to watch the birth of one child to weep over His design and order. What really makes me pick my jaw up off the floor is that He institutes that intentionality into our relationship with Him! How many times have you been teeth-grindingly frustrated with a circumstance God was taking you through, only to look back five years later and praise Him for His plan? God values process and order because they bring clarity. God often clarifies His love, intentionality and motives through a well-executed plan. Oftentimes, it is more than the end result God is after. He used the process to teach us why we had to go through what we went through. It is through the journey that He communicates what His core values are. Whether He is answering our prayer with "Yes", "No" or "Later", God often brings clarity through the process.

Now, I am aware that I am a little quirky when it comes to process. I am slightly obsessive over how dishes go into the dishwasher. When my wife wants something organized, she will make sure to mention in the flow of conversation, "Wow babe, you are really good at organizing closets". She knows that when she encourages me, I will gladly execute something else for her in a similar category. I need to have a clean and organized office to work efficiently. I always eat the salty before I eat the sweet, and nothing can be touching on my plate. I mean, are we animals?

I fully recognize this may not be you. I might have made a few of you nauseous just now with my description of how I like order and process. I would even go so far as to say that it would be sinful for me to tell you that you need to be like me when building a sermon. Throughout this whole book, I will press you to be yourself. I will say, however, you do need order and you do need a process. It is not that you *should* want a process or that it is somewhat helpful. You *need* a process. Process is critical for many reasons, but the main reason is that it helps the preacher work toward clarity. Often, when you short-cut process, you sacrifice clarity. If a preacher does not gain clarity for themselves, they will lose impact on their listeners. Process is also critical for longevity in preaching. If you don't allow process and consistency to be a staple for your sermon building, you will begin to say the same thing over and over and people will get tired of hearing that same story about your cat, or your same schtick about the Holy Spirit. They will tire of your circling back to that same application even though the Scripture should lead you to something new. Finally, process and structure are critical to your creativity and Holy Spirit invitation. I know that may seem contrary to the way you have been thinking, so let's start there.

Process Informs More Holy Spirit Invitation and Creativity

Often, preachers fear that establishing a process will cause them to lose the art of preaching. You fear you will lose your passion, which might cause you to abandon the persistent and desperate prayer for a word from the Lord because you have nothing for Sunday morning and its already Saturday night. The fear is that you may even lose your ability to let the Holy Spirit tweak and toy with your sermon. For some of you, process and order means sacrificing your heart. I understand that fear.

Preaching is much more of an art than science. However, I also believe that every good artist understands the science behind his art. Every good scientist also understands the art behind their science If a scientist does not have an ability to take risks and play around a little with their hypothesis, they may never have a breakthrough. If an artist does not set up their canvas in a place of inspiration or learn to create at the time of day that brings the most creative momentum, they will not be the artist they could be.

Structure and process are actually catapults to your creativity and Holy Spirit awareness. It starts with rhythm and expectation. Take a hypothetical walk with me as we consider the rhythm of sermon preparation. It is hypothetical because ownership of the sermon-building process is always more important than shoplifting someone else's. Suppose your rhythm for sermon preparation begins every Monday with prayerfully sitting down with the Scriptures and starting the process of exegesis. That rhythm puts you in a quiet place with the expectation that the Scriptures are moving and breathing. That is a biblical expectation. That also jump starts the creative sermonic juices flowing, and even when you are apart from the Scriptures, they will be on your mind, shaping thought. Maybe your rhythm has you crafting an outline by Tuesday, and your hermeneutics are in full swing. God is moving in your heart as you think about how context connects to culture. Faces, stories and empathy are highlighted at this stage. Maybe you start putting meat on the outline bones or you start writing your manuscript on Thursday because Wednesday is your notorious meeting day. All of your passions for people and the Scriptures are coming together as you think about how this one sermon can be a game changer for someone. These rhythms and healthy expectations have you pressing into God in a way that you wouldn't if you had no structure or process. The structure helps you listen and wait in a quiet place, aware of the Holy Spirit, with room to create most days out of the week as opposed to just a few days.

Think about your sermon like a house. Every house on my street is different. I love my street for that fact. There are no cookie cutter model houses lined up in a row. I have a house on my street (I have now moved from the city and live in Ohio) that looks like it belongs in the woods of Oregon and another house that looks like a one-level from southern California. I would call my street a creative street. If you drove around my neighborhood, you would think to yourself, "Either these are a bunch of different builders, or there is one builder with a lot of creativity". Either way, the creative process was never stymied. All these houses began the same way… process and structure. They all began with blueprints, permits and laying a solid foundation. Next, the houses were framed. They were all framed differently, and the blueprints were all different, but those houses had the same elements, nonetheless. The consistency of the process is what allowed room to create. The solid structural foundations are what allowed the dream of that house to come to life.

I am a Holy Spirit guy. In chapter 8, we will address how preachers divorced from a good pneumatology are also divorced from sustained and powerful preaching. Multiple times a year, the Holy Spirit, on Saturday, will impress upon me to change my sermon, a sermon that I have poured 12-14 hours into. I will listen and I will walk up there with just a few notes and pour out what God has given me. One Hundred Percent of my sermons get altered in the middle of the delivery. I might add an illustration that I felt God bring to my attention. I might hold back a few sentences that I feel would do more harm than good. I allow the Holy Spirit to shape and mold my creativity and my spontaneity so He can prophesy through me. But this could not happen apart from structure and process. The foundation and ideas are set through my exegesis and study of the Scriptures. The sermonic architectural drawings are laid out through my hermeneutics and homiletics. Holy Spirit invitation is happening at every point along the building process. Monday, the Holy Spirit has room to come alive in the Scriptures just as much as the Spirit has room in my final run through on Sunday. We can keep in step with the Spirit just as much in our diligence as we can in our manufactured desperation.

Process Informs Clarity

Having a process is also how you can be sure you have clarity. Clarity is what most new preachers struggle with the most. I can't tell you how many times I have sat in a preaching class trying to prevent the confusion in my brain from spreading to my face. A new preacher has endured thousands of sermons and thought to themselves, "I can do that." There are even times where they pull off a decent pulpit presence and a compelling delivery. But if they have no process, they have no clarity. Everyone is left wondering why they thought teaching 40 Scriptures in one sermon was a good idea. Folks are curious as to how this preacher got from point A to point J without any letters in between. Once your own lack of clarity has birthed confusion in your listeners, you have lost your ability to influence. A confused and cluttered mind has very little space to experience the power of God. Please understand, I'm not saying that you must follow my process for sermon preparation and construction. I am saying that having a process and owning it will make you a clearer preacher.

Process Informs Longevity

If you don't have a process, you will not have longevity in your preaching. I had someone come up to me once and tell me that they were bored of their preacher. They weren't really getting much out of his sermons anymore. I told them, "Of course you are not, you have been listening to them for 13 years!" I thought it was impressive that the attention lasted that long. I know preachers like to think that we will be compelling for 40 years and everyone will be sitting on the edge of their seat waiting for our next sentence. The reality is, if you don't have process, you won't morph; if you don't morph, you will have the same format, the same stories and the same flow. This formula ultimately results in your listeners having a hard time exploring new avenues of sanctification.

Process that leads to self-discovery will remedy this. You will need to write into your process elements of self-discovery and Holy Spirit discovery. An example of self-discovery is when someone manuscripts a sermon, a form of sermon writing I will go into later. They will naturally see places in their sermon where they are repetitive or redundant. Because of process, they will notice habits, pits of dullness and idiosyncrasies. One could not notice this or other urgent issues like a misunderstanding of Scripture or a bad source if they don't have a good, consistent process. An example of Holy Spirit discovery is when a preacher etches Holy Spirit time into their process. Time every week where they will listen to God. A time where they will soak in Scripture or a time where they will have no agenda. I used to walk around a dark sanctuary, sometimes for an hour at a time, just pacing in the presence of God. This is a time where God gives your heart ownership. He will ask you to repent before you tell others to do the same. Maybe God will bring you to other corresponding Scriptures or a broken reality in your own life that helps you connect to what He wants you to preach. Giving room to this in your process will help you have life changing moments of Holy Spirit discovery.

The Value of Ownership Over Your Own Process

I was at a conference where a pastor named John Stumbo, now the president of my denomination, the Christian and Missionary Alliance, said something that has affected me and my preaching for many years: "Be the most sanctified version of you." I was young enough in my preaching journey where that wisdom vibrated immediately because I wasn't trying to be myself in the pulpit. I was, at the time, trying to be a composite of four other people. I wasn't just listening to other preachers; I was trying to rent their process as well. I would listen to a podcast on their preparation, and I would try to duplicate that. Again, the major flaw in that is that I am not trying to be the most sanctified version of me, I am trying to be someone else. For instance, I heard a story about Mark Driscoll, previous to his fall from American Christian grace. Then, he was still a part of Acts 29. He was the pastor of one of the fastest growing churches in America. His Bible teaching was impacting American Christianity in an astronomical way. I was told that he mentioned in an interview that he essentially has a photographic memory. If the story and his claims were true, then his internalization process was short! I am not Mark Driscoll. You are not either. My internalization process was quite long. In my "before Christ" days, I may have consumed a little too much marijuana and I am paying for it today! I am forgiven, but my memory is still facing the consequences. Driscoll also had a different staff, and possibly research help. I cannot rent his process; I must own my own. I must be the most sanctified version of Justin Thornton.

I have seen processes on a wide spectrum. I have seen preachers manuscript, outline, do both, and do one before the other. I have seen preachers spend three hours in prayer before they touch a laptop. I have seen preachers have totally different ideal creative periods. Some are most active in sermon creation in the morning, some at night. The reality is that creation takes mental alertness and excitement. You, preacher, have a few hours a day where you have more mental capacity and creativity. For me, I am lowest on the mental capacity scale at 3pm after a burrito. If the scale is one out of ten, I am registering at a solid 1 in that moment. However, I register at a ten at 8 a.m. with a coffee and some Jesus music. I know people who have ideal creative periods at 10pm. You will have an ideal creative period. You will also develop an ideal process with tools that help, and ideal rhythms that will be unique to you. Some preachers I know use five commentaries to check their exegesis, some wouldn't touch a commentary with a ten-foot pole. Some take four hours in sermon prep and others take 20. Some are highly deductive in their creative process, and some are highly inductive. I think this is a beautiful reality and we should embrace that God created us like fingerprints. Each one has so much complexity and unique design that it becomes a futile exercise to imitate another. Our only option is to lean into the Holy Spirit and let the Good Teacher teach us what process might give us clarity and rhythm. What rhythm will match our specific role as pastor and what rhythm will eventually allow room for growth? Let God inform what process might help us connect better every week to the heart of God and our audience simultaneously.

As long as you have ownership over process, and that ownership embraces individualism and self-awareness, you will always have the ability grow into a better preacher every year. You will find impact not just in those you share the Word of God with, but also in your inner man or woman. You will learn who God made you to be and what tendencies He gave you. Play the long game and discover your process.

The Two Struggles

This process that you are close to entering addresses the two great struggles of new preachers: faithfulness to the text and faithfulness to clarity. The efforts to be faithful to the text and clarity can be straining and can, at times, feel like a mountain to climb. This mountain is a worthy climb. It is not for the corner-cutters or for the lazy, but it is for those who deeply value the Scriptures and deeply value preaching. If at any point your legs get tired or you feel famished, return to those things you value most. What do you value? Do you value a clear and faithful message? If you do, then keep moving your feet toward this process. As we enter the process that will take you from exegesis to the pulpit, make pit stops along the way to remind your heart how critical this really is.

Discussion and Practice

1. What about your current process is hindering your ability to be faithful to clarity in the pulpit?

_____
_____
_____
_____
_____
_____

2. What about your current process is hindering your ability to be faithful to the Text in the process of preaching?

_____
_____
_____
_____
_____
_____

3. Write out your current weekly process below so that it can be revisited and refined as you make progress throughout the book. (Example—Monday: Pray from 9-10am, Tuesday: Start read through of the Scripture.)

Monday-

Tuesday-

Wednesday-

Thursday-

Friday-

Saturday-

Sunday-

4. What needs to change about your current weekly rhythm?

_____

_____

_____

_____

_____

_____

CHAPTER 4
ORDER MATTERS

As a father of three, I have assembled more toys than an elf at the North Pole. As someone who has lived in five different sized homes in 13 years, I have assembled more furniture and cussed more often than I care to count. Let me just apologize to Jesus now before we move on. For some reason, nothing slows down my sanctification like putting together a toy or assembling a piece of furniture. Whenever Anne orders something that requires, "some assembly," I start the mental prep. I don't just pray and ask for the self-control to not throw a tool or let an unclean word leave my lips, but I pray for the reminder that *order matters*.

It is only after this sanctifying moment that I then take the wretched box full of 3,098 pieces, open it and discard the garbage. This is a critical step; I must have a clean workspace that is absent of clutter. Next, I turn on Sports Center and make sure all the small humans who populate my life are in a separate room. After that, I lay out every item and every tool, giving each item its own designated space. What follows is the most critical step of all… I read the instructions and follow them step by step! Now, I know that the ladies reading this book may have to pick their jaw off the floor because they were under the deep impression that men do not read instructions. Contrary to story told by many American sitcoms, I am fully dependent on instructions. I learned how critical the instructions are because, in my robust experience of assembly, I have ruined multiple items. I have added multiple hours of pain and insecurity. I have wasted many a scream and sigh due to going out of order. When you go out of order and when you underestimate the importance of order, you will always build something that is broken.

Now, the stakes are not exceptionally high when assembling a piece of IKEA furniture. I think their meatballs are better than their furniture anyway. However, the stakes are tremendously high when building a sermon. The stakes are clarity of God's intention, theological orthodoxy and the spiritual well-being of souls. Consider Paul's words to Timothy. He is urging Timothy to remain in Ephesus to confront the false teaching that exists there. There are teachers getting caught up in genealogies and teaching false doctrines. Their motives aren't clean, and their teaching is suspect. Paul says,

"The aim of our charge is love that issues from a pure heart and a good conscience and a sincere faith. Certain persons, by swerving from these, have wandered away into vain discussion, desiring to be teachers of the law, without understanding either what they are saying or the things about which they make confident assertions" (1 Timothy 1:5-7, ESV).

Paul is pleading the stakes. He is teaching Timothy that these teachers don't have the correct heart of the doctrine they are proclaiming, and they have a false interpretation. This is a dangerous mixture that will lead souls astray from correct relationship with Jesus. Those are the stakes. You could misrepresent the motives of God. You could bring an earthquake to the foundations of someone's understanding of God. You could lead God's sheep to a cliff or even a den of wolves.

Take just a moment and picture the people to whom you preach. Allow the weight of this responsibility, this calling, to settle over you— the weight of a lost world, the weight of correctly interpreting God's Word. This weight is not meant to be crushing or fear inducing but to lead us to reverence and sobriety. It is meant to remind us of the sacredness of the task. It should not result in pride but in humility, not timidity but boldness, not flippancy but care and faithfulness.

Order matters and the stakes are high. Your process will be your process. It will be as unique as a snowflake. It will be different than your preaching mentor's or your favorite podcast preacher. However, there are some elements of the process that are non-negotiables and will set the tone for your preaching. They will determine whether you are preaching the Word of God or tickling ears. They will determine whether you are constructing this sermon in reverence to Jesus or reverence to human opinion. Whether you will preach resurrection life messages or anemic TED talks. Maybe you have sat through thousands of sermons and only a few of them had real punch. Maybe you look at the landscape of preaching like a predominately CGI movie. It looks and sounds really good, but there is nothing of real substance to it. Preaching now leaves the soul wanting. It isn't like the 21st century invented impotent preaching. Dietrich Bonhoeffer was dealing with the same false teaching in his day. In Eric Metaxas' biography of Bonhoeffer, he quotes a letter written about Bonhoeffer's time in America[12].

"The sermon has been reduced to parenthetical church remarks about newspaper events. As long as I've been here, I have heard only one sermon in which you could hear something like a genuine proclamation…. In New York they preach about virtually everything; only one thing is not addressed, or is addressed so rarely that I have as yet been unable to hear it, namely, the gospel of Jesus Christ, the cross, sin and forgiveness, death and life".

Does that sound familiar? Have you ever left a worship service and felt like you just left a sushi restaurant? Everything looked good, and at times you even felt like you might be full after the meal, but there was so much rice and so little protein that you left hungry and lacking nutrients. Why is that? Well, the answer is simple; from the beginning, the message you heard was not coming from the word of God. The preacher's process started in the wrong place. There was not a core belief that it was the Word of God that breathed life into the very bones of people. The core belief was that there needed to be a well-constructed sermon. This is a lie that much of American Christianity has purchased and therefore our sermons lack depth and

---

[12] Metaxas, Eric. *Bonhoeffer: Pastor, Martyr, Prophet, Spy.* Nelson Books, Nashville, TN, 2010, 2020, pp 54.

substance. Eventually, we will find that our disciples have also become shallow and insubstantial. We will. Again, the stakes are high and order matters.

The Science and Practice of Interpretation

Let me introduce a word that maybe you have never heard—hermeneutics. Hermeneutics is *the study of sciences and practices in interpretation.* This could mean the study of interpretation as it pertains to many fields, but specific to our purposes, biblical hermeneutics is the study of interpretation of the Bible.

Most of the interpretive process I will unpack in this chapter will fit in a nice, linear pattern. Hermeneutics is like a bully who shows up to a linear pool party and does a cannon ball. There is an ongoing argument between those who try to force hermeneutics either before or after exegesis, and those who think that hermeneutics floats above exegesis, inserting itself in the process at appropriate times. I tend to agree with the latter. It is only a tendency, though; unlike most arguments, this one doesn't really have an ending and both parties are right in a sense. For the purposes of clarity and simplicity, one of my core values in writing this book, I am going to argue for one side and stick to it.

If Hermeneutics is *the study of sciences and practices in interpretation…*

Exegesis is *the actual interpretation.*

This is a subtle important difference. While hermeneutics is the study and science of how to interpret the Bible, exegesis is the act of interpretation. I found the best description in a forum[13];

---

[13] *What is the difference between exegesis and hermeneutics?* [online] Biblical Hermeneutics Stack Exchange. 2021. Available at: hermeneutics.stackexchange.com/questions/36/what-is-the-difference-between-exegesis-and-hermeneutics.

"So we are sort of comparing apples to... ontology here. In a sense there is no overlap; The focus of exegesis is the text. The focus of hermeneutics is stuff like exegesis... why do we do it? how do we do it? how should we do it? As far as sequence, I suppose it would be argued that since exegesis is "critical" in nature, it implies some scientific method, which implies some prior hermeneutic. That is as far as I think we could go in relating the two sequentially, though".

I am simple-minded and desire pictures and exercises when trying to grasp the complex ideas of processes. To aid with understanding, I will give you both in this chapter.

What if I were to tell you that someone texted someone else, "I went into a bank with a mask on and demanded money." Now if you were not in interpreting mode and you were in assumption mode, your assumption would lead you to a few conclusions: 1. That person is going to go to jail or, 2. That person is going to be on the run for a very long time and the recipient is now an accessory to bank robbery. But let's go into interpretation mode together. Text messages are notorious for lacking context and tone. Assumption is usually unhelpful. The same goes for biblical interpretation. You will want to ask a few questions like:

1. Who is sending this text?
2. Where is the person who is texting?
3. When are they texting?
4. What is the tone?

By using these questions, you would be applying a good hermeneutic to the process of interpretation. In your study of the science of text message interpretation, you have learned to ask these questions. That is hermeneutics. You can use the science of interpretation not just on the Scriptures but also on the culture within which we now live, and when connecting those two contexts. That is why I don't believe in looking at this process as necessarily sequential. Hermeneutics will positively interrupt throughout your process. Let's apply exegesis or the actual interpretation to those same questions.

1. The people texting are friends.
2. The people texting are in New York City.
3. The people are texting in the year 2020 during a global pandemic, and masks are mandated inside of banks.
4. The tone is joking between friends.

Here is a diagram that I believe will help figure out where hermeneutics actually fits in your process and order:

Exegesis

Exegesis & Hermeneutics

Hermeneutics - Study of sciences and practices in interpretation.
Exegesis- Actual Interpretation

Hermeneutics

Exegesis   Application from ancient   Homiletical Structure
            culture to todays culture

As you can see, exegesis and hermeneutics are not in competition with each other, they are comrades. One doesn't always come before another but using a good hermeneutic throughout your process will always be necessary.

Discussion and Practice

1. Have there been Scriptures which, when well explained, you have realized you have been misinterpreting for years? If so, which ones?

_____
_____
_____
_____
_____
_____

2. What elements of hermeneutics will you apply from now on when interpreting the Scriptures? (Example: I will research the author's motivation for the Scripture)

_____
_____
_____
_____
_____
_____

3. What elements of hermeneutics will you apply when interpreting the culture you are preaching to?

_____
_____
_____
_____
_____
_____

4. Write out your own metaphor or teaching tool that will help you distinguish between hermeneutics and exegesis.

_____

_____

_____

_____

_____

_____

CHAPTER 5
EXEGESIS

To understand exegesis, you must understand its longstanding nemesis, eisegesis. It is a bit like understanding Batman better through understanding The Joker. Understanding the motives of one enables you to understand the minutest idiosyncrasies of the other. Maybe a tree is a more accessible metaphor. If you look at a tree at the peak of fall standing amongst other trees, you will certainly see its beauty. However, there is another level of beauty to stand in awe of when you place that tree next to a dead tree.

Sometimes, a thing's beauty is more easily seen when sitting in contrast to its counterpart. The goodness of Batman is best apprehended in light of The Joker's malice. The beauty of a majestic oak in full fall-color is most striking when seen in contrast to the bent and dead, dark gray birch standing in its shadow.

As we move forward, let's define both exegesis and eisegesis and give a few examples of each.

Exegesis vs. Eisegesis

Exegesis (OUT OF)-is the process of drawing the original meaning— in its original context—and the authorial intention *out of* the text.

Everything in that definition is critical! The author's intention is critical. The context, meaning the city, time-period and cultural implications are all critical. We are studying a book made up of 66 books that have been written by about 35 authors over a time-period that exceeds one-thousand years. Yes, we must not forget the divine author. The Holy Spirit is the inspiration and primary author of the Scriptures. But God also very intentionally used humans to write this book that would be carried into wildly different times, spaces, and cultures. The most critical words, however, in that definition are, *"out of"*. It is the essence of exegesis to study and pull the meaning *out of*, and not bring meaning *into* the text.

Eisegesis (INTO)-is the process of reading meaning and intention *into* the text.

In other words, exegesis allows the Scriptures to impose their will on you while eisegesis imposes your will on the Scriptures. There is always a starting point. and often how you start will determine how you finish. If you start with eisegesis, most often you will end up with a sermon based around your ideas and what you hope God would say. If you start with exegesis, and you commit to saying faithfully whatever God seems to be saying in the text, then you will end up with a faithful and powerful message from the mouth of God.

There was once a preacher, and he was in the shower thinking through his next sermon series. As he applied soap to his washcloth, he had a brilliant idea: "What if I talked about money? Our church is a little broke right now and a money series would really help." Next, he thought about the one-liner he heard the other day when listening to his favorite preacher. "If it's God's will, it's God's bill!" He gave a Holy Spirit grunt and then began thinking through his head catalogue of Bible passages that may support this fantastic one-liner. He couldn't think of much yet, but at least he had his title. "God's will, God's bill." It's clean and punchy. He could picture it on social media, with clouds and some trees in the background of this catchy text. He could think of a time where he felt like God paid for something that his family needed. "Bang! I already have the first page of this week's sermon!". Our preacher thought to himself, "I will find the right Bible passage later." Since most of our Holy Spirit inspiration comes in the car or in the shower, he was in the car when he was inspired by the first Bible passage that came to mind:

"Bring the full tithe into the storehouse, that there may be food in my house. And thereby put me to the test, says the Lord of hosts, if I will not open the windows of heaven for you and pour down for you a blessing until there is no more need." Malachi 3:9-10.

"That's it! There is my main passage. This week's sermon could be about how if we trust God and tithe, He will open the flood gates and pay for it all. If it is His will, it is His bill".

Maybe you can sense just a few of the eisegetical land mines our preacher may step on.

Land Mine 1- *His main truth is disjointed.* The main truth he is trying to communicate is in two parts and has a slight fracture. *This week's sermon could be about how if we trust God and tithe, he will open the flood gates and pay for it all. If it is His will, it is His bill".* It is subtle, but his first truth is about trusting in God's provision and his second truth is centered on God's will. This micro fracture will lead to a confused outline and therefore a confused crowd. Remember, a lack of clarity translates to a lack of power.

Land Mine 2- *His main truth is disjointed from God's main truth.*
God's main truth here is that He wants His people to return to Him and His covenant. Part of His covenant with them is that they would bring their tithes and offerings to the storehouse. This comes from a deep understanding that nothing is ours, we are only stewards of what God owns. This preacher is on a dangerous path toward preaching something that God did not intend to be preached out of this particular interaction with His people. I am not saying he is a heretic, but he is staring at the heretic lunch table, and he is thinking about sitting down.

Land Mine 3- *He is in danger of teaching a descriptive Scripture in a prescriptive manner.* This is a descriptive Scripture about a certain people in relationship with God at a specific time with an elaborate and specific history. While there may be some prescriptive principles in this text, e.g., repentance, idolatry and trusting God, this is not a prescriptive text about tithing.

Land Mine 4- *He is in danger of an anemic sermon.* This sermon, while having a few catchy and tweetable one-liner's will be human centric. The core of it will be a human idea and therefore the outer layers will be mostly human ideas and illustrations. It will lack the punch and the right hook of the Holy Spirit. This is perhaps one of the major reasons you have sat through many a sermon and felt like there just was no blood flow there.

I have only named a few possible land mines in this parable. And before we move on, I would like to address a question I get asked consistently when teaching preachers how to preach: "Is it wrong have an idea about what to preach and have a Scripture in your heart to match?" In other words, if you have been studying the Scriptures and have those Scriptures written on your heart, isn't the core of your idea, the Holy Spirit's inspiration? Can't one harmlessly come before the other? Absolutely! But let me talk about *"The Line"*

The Exegesis Line- If your inspiration comes from somewhere else besides sitting down and going through the Scriptures verse by verse, you will undoubtedly in your sermon building process approach *The Exegesis Line*. This is the moment where you decide whether you are going to impose your will on the Scriptures or allow the Scriptures to impose God's will on your sermon. This is typically a choice before your sermon prep begins. You will make a decision to empty all of yourself and come to a primary Scripture, waiting for God to reveal through prayer and study what the text is saying, or you will come with an illustration you thought of that week and let that drive the sermon.

Maybe there is a moment in your building where you think of a nice corresponding Scripture, but instead of taking the time to check into that Scripture, you just assume the last guy who preached it had it right, so you decide to do a flyover. While the line is most often at the front end of your building process, it can be nuanced all throughout the process, especially if you are building a topical sermon. Therefore, let me say it like this: the exegesis line is like an abstract painting, often the artist only knows the intention. There will be a moment where you have a choice to do the work and make the original intention of the original author in its original context a priority before you cross the bridge to today's culture.

Enemies of Exegesis

I would like to give you three poor attitudes to exegesis that put you in danger of being behind enemy lines. And if you feel like these metaphors are all a bit aggressive and you are wondering why there is so much battle rhetoric, I will just point out that there is a war for the soul of your sermon, and the soul of your people. Ephesians 6:17 gives you an offensive weapon of choice, "*and take the helmet of salvation, and the sword of the Spirit, which is the word of God*".

Hebrews 4:12 explains its power to reach into the soul of humanity: "*For the word of God is living and active, sharper than any two-edged sword, piercing to the division of soul and of spirit, of joints and of marrow, and discerning the thoughts and intentions of the heart.*" In other words, I know your title was really catchy and that illustration about the car motor was the best you heard in a while but stop walking up to the pulpit with a pool noodle. Pick up your sword.

Enemy 1. Laziness- There was once a Pastor on a golf course with a friend of mine. On the back nine on a Thursday, he had a revelation. He had not yet put together his sermon for Sunday. Oh drat! He proceeded to call his assistant and notify her that she needed to go into his desk and locate one of the many Charles Spurgeon sermons that he had tucked away, pull it out and put it on his desk. This is a true story, and has so much laziness attached to it, it is comical. I mean, brother, you are so lazy, you couldn't even pull that sermon out yourself. You had your assistant play Russian roulette inside your desk of plagiarism?

Enemy 2. Priority- Let's go back to chapter 1. Priority is an immediate product of value. If you are having priority issues, it may be a good time to go back and read Chapters 1 and 2. Maybe it would be a helpful exercise to do a study throughout the Scriptures on what God thinks of the proclamation of His word. It might be a value issue, but it could also be an organizational competence issue as well. Exegesis is often one of the first priorities to be pushed off to the side when ministry inevitably becomes too busy and sometimes the Pastor simply doesn't know how to organize the ministry in such a way that will make his or her preaching a high value again. The Early Church wrestled with a similar issue. The widows and orphans were not being taken care of and so they had to get around the table and make some decisions.

"And the twelve summoned the full number of the disciples and said, 'It is not right that we should give up preaching the word of God to serve tables. Therefore, brothers, pick out from among you seven men of good repute, full of the Spirit and of wisdom, whom we will appoint to this duty. But we will devote ourselves to prayer and to the ministry of the word." (Acts 6:2-4, ESV).

Verse two makes the disciples come off like a bunch of brats who won't get their hands dirty, but verse three brings it all home. They don't just pick anyone for this important task, they pick people with good repute and full of the Spirit. I am sure you know that the famous martyr, Stephen, is among them. They are simply saying both elements are important, therefore, let us raise up a team to handle care for the widows and orphans while we dedicate our time to prayer and the ministry of the word. Make a decision today to raise up and empower teams around you so you can devote yourself to the exegesis and preaching of the Scriptures.

Enemy 3. Assumption- How old were you when you found out that your favorite T-shirt verse was about a people living in exile under their mortal enemy? Jeremiah 29:11 is a banner verse of acontextual encouragement. How old were you when you realized that Job 1 was not an every morning prescriptive interaction between God and Satan? For years you thought every time someone suffered, Satan got the quick go ahead from God. We assume that it has been preached correctly to us time and time again. Instead of doing the work ourselves, we glide up to the pulpit and parrot what we heard from our favorite preacher. The future preacher sitting in the audience will repeat your mistake. This is how we preach a verse out of context for decades upon decades.

A Simple Process

Over the years, the word "Exegesis" has become an inaccessible idea for aspiring preachers. It feels like it is only for scholars and if you attempt to make exegesis a priority, you will always be hanging over a cliff of heresy. You aren't smart enough and you haven't read through the entire Bible enough times to exegete. This is simply not true, but order does matter, and the first element will continue to prepare your heart for what is next.

Prayer

The cup needs to be emptied and clean before it is available to be filled. We often come to the Scriptures in a hurry, broken, prideful and angry. We approach the breath of God with angst and anxiety. We have people's names and faces bouncing around in our heads and we have grudges to settle. We have our own background and culture to deal with, let alone the Scriptures. That is a lot to bring *into* the text. Remember, the goal is to extract God's meaning *out of*, not bring our meaning *into* the text. The moment of prayer before you start your exegesis process is as critical as any other moment in your sermon-building. This is your time to empty the cup. It is a time to check your luggage before boarding. It is also the time to invite the supernatural. Do you believe that God is supernaturally chasing people? Do you believe that when the Holy Spirit fills a preacher and fills a room full of people that the supernatural can happen? Do you believe that God's Word is true and that there is instance after instance of the supernatural when the supernatural is invited through a humbled prophet? One of the core values of my denomination, the Christian and

Missionary Alliance, is "Prayer is the primary work of God's people". That idea is antagonistic to our fleshly inclinations. We want to control first (what we see as work) and pray second. I dare you to try sermon building the other way around and watch God move. Invite God to go first. Invite God to deal with you first. Invite God to empty you and then fill you again with His Word.

Who

You will need to discover who the original author is and who the original audience were. This is not as simple as writing them down on a sheet of paper. Let's pretend you and I are friends. That sounds really nice. I like friends and so do you. Let's also pretend that we went to a grocery store together—that is how good our relationship is. We are grocery store shopping level friends. At the store, we see someone, and you elude, while looking in their direction, that you may have known them. I would then say to you, "Who are they?" If you simply told me their name, I would promptly ask for more. I am asking for the back story. If I am really interested, I want cultural details, family members and character history. That's what I am asking for when I say, "Who are they?" When you sit down to discover "the who," you are looking for all the elements that make up a people and all the elements that make up an author. This information will not just help you avoid being a heretic, but it will also help give your sermon color.

Let's use 1 Corinthians 9:24 as an example. *"Do you not know that in a race all the runners run, but only one receives the prize? So run that you may obtain it"* (ESV).

The audience is clearly the Church at Corinth. But that is about as much color as a 50's television sitcom. That is not *who* they are. Let's discover *who* they are in light of the author's topic. The Greeks were obviously the catalysts and initiators of the Olympic games. Historians can trace the first games back to 776 BC in Olympia. The sanctuary of Poseidon at Isthmia was located within the territory of the city of Corinth. Attached to the sanctuary were athletic games that were held every two years. The center focus of these games was the track events. That gives your listeners a bit of context that will help them understand how the first hearers in Corinth would have understood "the race" our author is speaking of.

What about the context of the prize? Yes, it is common knowledge that only one gets a prize in a race, but let's really add some color, shall we? The original event in this context was called "the Stadion". It was a race of 192 meters and if you won this event, there was a chance you would have your name attached to the games until the next meet. You would probably also have your statue cast in bronze and installed at the venue. The prize was significant. Paul's original audience is a competitive people who make this running event significant year in and year out. Having a deep understanding of "the who"—to people to whom the scriptural author is writing— helps you add dimension and color in a way that you simply wouldn't if you don't do the research. It helps you teleport into the mind and heart of the original audience so that you can build a case in the court of meaning.

What about the author? Yes, this one is easy because Paul announces himself at the beginning of the book of 1 Corinthians. I love when they do that. But what about Paul is significant for this Scripture? If we contextualize Paul a bit, we know that he runs the spiritual race with grit and perseverance. He will experience more hardships than most any human being we come into contact with. His zeal is well documented, even before he meets Jesus on the road to Damascus. He crosses the finish line serving Jesus all the way up to and through martyrdom. This metaphor is deeply significant to him and to his audience. This is information that you need to obtain. Make sure you study "the who".

What

You also need to answer two major questions in the category of *what.* These questions will immediately tie into your homiletical structure. The first question is *what* is the *Principal Truth* the author is trying to communicate? There is not always just one truth and often you are dealing with a passage and that passage could have multiple truths lying within it. Often, Paul will really give preachers a headache and he will start spraying truth bullets around like a pre- pubescent boy with a nerf gun. Take 2 Timothy 2:22-26:

"So flee youthful passions and pursue righteousness, faith, love, and peace, along with those who call on the Lord from a pure heart. Have nothing to do with foolish,

ignorant controversies; you know that they breed quarrels. And the Lord's servant must not be quarrelsome but kind to everyone, able to teach, patiently enduring evil, correcting his opponents with gentleness. God may perhaps grant them repentance leading to a knowledge of the truth, and they may come to their senses and escape from the snare of the devil, after being captured by him to do his will." (ESV)

Many a preacher are like Doug, the dog from the movie "Up" and have "Squirrel Syndrome". They are excited about one idea in this passage until, "Squirrel!" they become fixated on another idea. They started really digging into the idea of "youthful passions" when "ignorant controversies" stole their attention and before they know it, their sermon has more topics than a game of Charades.

The anchor here is that we are looking for the *"Principal Truth"*. The word "principal" means *a fundamental truth or proposition that serves as the foundation for a system of belief or behavior or for a chain of reasoning.* We are looking for the fundamental and foundational truth of the passage. In the case of 2 Timothy 2, Paul is shooting rapid fire because he is explaining the characteristic of a good worker, a good servant, of Christ. That is the Principal Truth and that is what the sermon needs to be built upon.

The preacher must keep looking for the Principal Truth because it will give context to the rest of the truth that lies within the passage. Look at it like a headline of a news article. The headline of a news article aims to sum up all the elements of the events and draw out the Principal Truth of all that follows. The writer will labor over that headline not only because they need something to grip the reader's attention, but also their discipline of discovering the Principal Truth will help bring clarity and color to the rest of the truth within that article. Many topics loom within the news article. There may even be a significant temptation to choose another headline, even if it is another topic. But it is the skill and discipline to choose the Principal Truth that gives the article foundational integrity. Your discovery and labor over the wording of your Principal Truth will give your sermon foundational integrity and clarity. Most of all, it will line the heart of your sermon up with the heart of the Author.

I will tease out the Principal Truth much further in chapter 6 but for now, you may be wondering, "How do I look for the Principal Truth?" I will admit that, often, it feels like you are arguing with a spouse. The one thing that keeps coming to mind is, "What are you actually trying to say?"

You are not unusual if the Principal Truth doesn't just jump straight off of the page. Here are a few questions I found helpful when trying to discover the Principal Truth.

1. Is there an umbrella? Sometimes in your search, you are not looking for a key phrase or a sentence that sticks out, you are looking for an umbrella idea. An idea that sits at 30,000 feet above all the topics below. I know that's a really tall umbrella, but you get the point. I will give you a passage of Scripture as an example. I think it would be cherry picking to pick one of Paul's writings because of his very deductive reasoning type of writing. He often states his Principal Truth at the beginning of one of his rants. Instead, let's choose a narrative passage from the Old Testament because this type of literature often makes it much more difficult to find the umbrella truth.

We have to keep in mind that the Old Testament writers were telling a story —a story with Principal Truth they were trying to communicate. They were not preaching; they were not writing a letter to a New Testament Church plant; they were simply telling a story. Therefore, this will not be as cut and dried as you cut and dry folks may like. This is why we invite the Holy Spirit and do the work. That is what will help us rest at night. The discernment of the Holy Spirit as we walk through a book that the Spirit authored with careful labor and balanced study will get us where we need to go. Here is the passage:

"Moreover, from the time that I was appointed to be their governor in the land of Judah, from the twentieth year to the thirty-second year of Artaxerxes the king, twelve years, neither I nor my brothers ate the food allowance of the governor. The former governors who were before me laid heavy burdens on the people and took from them for their daily ration forty shekels of silver. Even their servants lorded it over the people. But I did not do so, because of the fear of God. I also persevered in the work on this wall, and we acquired no land, and all my servants were gathered there for the work. Moreover, there were at my table 150 men, Jews and officials, besides those who came to us from the nations that were around us. Now what was prepared at my expense for each day was one ox and six choice sheep and birds, and every ten days all kinds of wine in abundance. Yet for all this I did not demand the food allowance of the governor, because the service was too heavy on this people. Remember for my good, O my God, all that I have done for this people." (Nehemiah 5: 14-19, ESV)

Again, there is a lot of truth in this passage. You can pluck any one of those truths out of this passage and turn it into a sermon. You could talk about perseverance or generosity. Good truths, but you did not locate the umbrella truth. The umbrella truth which can be an umbrella topic for the whole passage in this passage is the healthy fear of God, in relationship with God leads you to character leadership. Since we have located the umbrella truth, we can talk about the character elements that come along with that fear and relationship as sub points. Is there an umbrella truth in your passage? That will lead you to the Principal Truth.

2. Is there repetition? Let's take Psalm 19 for example. There may not be one word that is said over and over again, but there is plenty of repetition to feast on:

"The **law** *of the Lord is perfect, reviving the soul; the* **testimony** *of the Lord is sure, making wise the simple; the* **precepts** *of the Lord are right, rejoicing the heart; the* **commandment** *of the Lord is pure, enlightening the eyes; the fear of the Lord is clean, enduring forever; the* **rules** *of the Lord are true, and righteous altogether. More to be desired are they than gold, even much fine gold; sweeter also than honey and drippings of the honeycomb"* (Psalm 19:7-10, ESV).

David uses his favorite words in repetition to talk about the commands and proclamation of God. Each word emboldened represents something David loves that precedes from the mouth and mind of God. For those three verses, David is using repetition to magnify the heart of God. Is there repetition in your passage? This will also help lead you to the Principal Truth.

The second major question you will need to answer in the category of *what* is, is there a *Principal Sin* present? You will have the temptation to look at the sins that present themselves as it pertains to your culture and your people. It is a natural bent of preachers to immediately target how people in the current context fall short of the glory of God according to the Principal Truth of a particular passage. However, I am not talking about the present culture and the present sin; we will save that investigation for the hermeneutics and homiletics portion of your sermon building. I am simply asking if is there a sin of the ancient people that is being pointed out or targeted within the passage. If there is a list of sins like the list in Romans 1:29-30, is there an umbrella character that is being pointed out? Is there a *Principal Sin* present? This will also carry over into your homiletical structure. Once you have targeted the Principal Truth and/or the Principal Sin, you have located your *what*.

Where

Where is the author? More importantly where is his audience? Again, a name like Colossae or Ephesus will very likely not be enough to give clarity and color to your sermon. You will need to find the texture and feel of ancient Ephesus if you want to place your listeners closer to the feelings in the room as Paul is writing the letter to the Ephesians. It will give you more accuracy to original intent and it will help you build a more compelling case throughout your sermon. The truth is, people not only want ancient context, but people also need ancient context if they are to understand the original authorial intent of the passage being investigated. It is intriguing and gripping to discover something new. Every story is a better story when the story is made as 3D as possible.

Now before you start to get cold sweats over how much work seems to be piling up, I would like to put your mind at ease. You will spend quite a bit of time on the *who, where,* and *when,* if you are starting a verse-by-verse sermon series on a book of the Bible. Most of that work can be done up front. I am certainly not saying you need to spend an hour on the where when you are just going to address one passage. If you are going to address a passage in a book, you will be wise to study the habits, idols and details surrounding that specific topic of that specific passage. In other words, what is the author talking about that would make for relevant study? Here is 1 Corinthians 10:7: *"Do not be idolaters as some of them were; as it is written, 'The people sat down to eat and drink and rose up to play'"* (ESV). The relevant topic at hand is clearly idolatry, and although Paul quotes Exodus here, he is also thinking about the idolatry of the Church in Corinth. If you study the idolatry in Corinth, you will find that the early Christians and their leaders were struggling with their people eating at temples and pagan festivals. They were even attending festivals at the Sanctuary of Poseidon and often there were animal sacrifices, and some of those sacrifices were consumed by the participants. Paul clearly has a specific motive to this command, and we have the tools to stay close to his motive and so will stay true to the text with a little care and intentionality.

When

Time period or the timing of the text can also play an important role when trying to exegete context. For example, when exegeting Mark 16:1-8, timing is absolutely critical. I will not be the first or last person to build this case, but the most pivotal moment in humanity just happened; Jesus has risen from the dead. All of Christianity hinges on whether or not Jesus rose from the dead. Because of that, the testimony of Jesus' resurrection and the witnesses who encounter the risen Christ and tell his story have supreme value. Who would Jesus tell? Who would He speak to first? Because Jesus would not appear to everyone at once, the timing of His first reveal is important.

"When the Sabbath was past, Mary Magdalene, Mary the mother of James, and Salome bought spices, so that they might go and anoint him. And very early on the first day of the week, when the sun had risen, they went to the tomb. And they were saying to one another, 'Who will roll away the stone for us from the entrance of the tomb?' And looking up, they saw that the stone had been rolled back—it was very large. And entering the tomb, they saw a young man sitting on the right side, dressed in a white robe, and they were alarmed. And he said to them, 'Do not be alarmed. You seek Jesus of Nazareth, who was crucified. He has risen; he is not here. See the place where they laid him. But go, tell his disciples and Peter that he is going before you to Galilee. There you will see him, just as he told you.' And they went out and fled from the tomb, for trembling and astonishment had seized them, and they said nothing to anyone, for they were afraid." (Mark 16:1-8, ESV)

Timing is critical here, not just because Jesus fulfills His prophecy and promise of rising from the dead in three days, but also because He revealed the most important information of all time to women first. Jesus was a game changer for women; He spoke to a Samaritan woman at a well, He involved women on His ministry team, and rebuked religious male leaders for worrying about money when the woman (most assume Mary) was anointing Jesus' feet. This would be another moment where Jesus intentionally revolutionizes the role women have in His Kingdom.

I love barbeque. Let me say it for you in the back, I love barbeque! A pulled pork sandwich with some coleslaw and some spicy pickles should go down in a hall of fame somewhere. I don't know which hall of fame, just take my word for it. Now picture a father on his death bed. His seven children surround him with tears in their eyes. This is not just a pivotal moment because their father is dying, but because he promised to share the most important ingredient to his barbeque sauce with the child that would carry on the family business. Jimmy's barbeque pit has carried the family legacy for four generations and this one ingredient is what separates Jimmy's barbeque from the rest of the competition. The seven children wait around with bated breath because that information will not just change their relationship with their dying father, but it will also give them a new life. They will lead the business, and life trajectory will surely change. Do you think timing of information and the intention of who receives this information first is important?

Now, I don't think we need to spend a lot of time scaling this up. The resurrected King is sharing the testimony of the most important event in history. Whom it goes to first is of utmost importance. This is followed by other exegetical factors, like the lack of validity society and the Pharisees gave to a woman's testimony and the overall platform of women in ancient Jewish society. The timing of this information has to play into the way you view women in ministry and preaching. Jesus is absolutely making a statement here through the when and "the who". It is not a favoritism statement, but it is a revolutionary statement, and it must play into how you view women in ministry and in the pulpit. It must play into your exegesis of other Scriptures as you let the Bible teach you the Bible. It also builds a strong case that timing can be critical in the text you are interpreting.

Literary Form

I heard an anecdote once. A man walks up to a pastor and asks the pastor, "Do you read the Bible literally?" Learning from Jesus to answer a question with a question, he replied, "Do you read the library literally?" The Bible contains 66 books over thousands of years. It contains many different eras and forms of literature. This may seem like obvious territory. We should not teach Poetic Literature as Historical literal, or Prophetic passages as Poetic, although sometimes our prophets do become poets and sometimes our poetry has historical information. The obvious application here is to teach the text, as it is. Teach a Poetic Book as a Poetic Book. The Author intended it as poetry and therefore uses metaphor and exaggeration. There is the cadence of a poem and so chronological and literal applications may not be the best interpretation. It is, however, good to first understand the metaphor, teach it as metaphor and then apply its properties as the author intended. Understanding the author's literary intention will help you teach what God desires you to teach. Take Genesis 1:1–3:24 for instance.

The question when reading Genesis 1:1-3:24 and every passage for that matter is, "What does God want me to get out of this and what does God want me to deliver?" The beginning of the Scriptures creates some problems in answering that question if we don't navigate through literary form. One may ask, how come it seems like Adam is created after the animals in Genesis 1:1-2:4 but then there is a shift in 2:4b-3:24 and it appears Adam is created first? Well, the answer is in the literary form. The umbrella narrative of the whole book, I think we can safely say, is narrative prose. Whereas Genesis 1:1-2:4 has a poetic cadence and has poetic timing. Our Author here, who most assume is Moses, is using two forms of literature. One form, the poetic form, is to give us an overall picture of the character, glory and power of God. His intentionality in creation is awe inspiring. The other form, narrative prose, is to give us God's view on man and woman and their place in creation.

If we teach this book as historical/literal and chronological in nature, we could easily end up arguing for centuries over how old the earth is, dinosaurs, a literal six-day creation and its implications. While I believe those discussions have their place, I am not sure they are the primary questions the text is answering.

Let's look at some more common mistakes when it comes to not understanding literary form or authorial intention.

Descriptive and Prescriptive Texts

One common mistake occurs when a preacher or teacher is teaching prescriptive texts as descriptive and descriptive texts as prescriptive. When studying the Bible, you will encounter two types of texts, descriptive and prescriptive. Descriptive texts are describing a place, time, and relational interaction between God and a people or person. In that moment, the Bible is describing and unpacking that historical moment—it is simply telling us what happened. Often, there is hyper specific detail of the context, a law given, or a command given. But that law or that command was for those people in that moment. It is descriptive of that context and time. In other words, just because God said it to a people wandering in the desert thousands of years ago, it doesn't mean He meant it to be applied in 21st century Western culture. Take Deuteronomy 24:10-11 for example:

"When you make your neighbor a loan of any sort, you shall not go into his house to collect his pledge. You shall stand outside, and the man to whom you make the loan shall bring the pledge out to you." (ESV)

Although I feel quite entertained thinking about the reader really wrestling with their integrity as they figure out whether they should go inside someone's house to collect a loan or just stand outside chucking rocks and yelling, it is reckless to teach this as a prescriptive text for today. Descriptive texts teach us a whole lot about God and his values but are not meant to be wielded as a command.

Prescriptive texts are just the opposite. They are commands from an interaction with God in the Scriptures that are meant to be applied until Jesus comes riding on the clouds. They are prescriptive in the same way that a doctor prescribes that you do not to take 40 Advil at a time. I think even scholars can agree that Matthew 28:19 and Acts 1:8 are a few prescriptive texts that we can safely teach as prescriptive.

Hyper-Comparison

There has been a change in preaching and worship music. The root of it, I believe, is the worship of self. Everything in this life, including preaching and worship, revolves around the wonderful axis of *you*. You can hear it in the subtle hints of a narrative in a worship song. At some point in the story of that song, you aren't sure if you are worshipping God or how much God thinks of you. This also plays out in preaching. We will take an ancient narrative about someone else, and we will apply *hyper-comparison*. All of a sudden, you are fighting Goliath and you are parting the seas or walking on water. We aren't positive who the hero is because although it's God's power that is doing the work, eventually your story takes center stage. God slides into a sidekick uniform and gives your narcissistic story legs. You become the champion and you can conquer anything. There is value in applying biblical narrative to our own, but we must be careful to not cross the line. The truth is we have not suffered like Job. Similarly, being swallowed by a fish will probably never be a part of our story. And while it is helpful to compare, there should be discernment in the language used and the measure applied.

Prayer

Yes, I know, I've already talked about prayer, but it is time to pray again. You have done the work of exegesis, and have done your best to interpret the work, now it is time to put an outline together. Ask God to be present and drive the process. Ask him to be alive in your preaching and bring to mind the burdens of your people. Ask Him for power and anointing. If your process is bathed in prayer, your sermon will be bathed in power.

Discussion and Practice

Take three Scriptures and fill in the blanks as you apply good hermeneutic while exegeting the Text.

Scripture 1

Who

_____

_____

_____

_____

_____

_____

_____

What

_____

_____

_____

_____

_____

_____

Where

_____

_____

_____

_____

_____

_____

When

_____

_____

_____

_____

_____
_____
_____

Literary Form

_____
_____
_____
_____
_____
_____
_____

Scripture 2

Who

_____
_____
_____
_____
_____
_____
_____

What

_____
_____
_____
_____
_____
_____
_____

Where

_____
_____
_____
_____
_____
_____
_____

When

_____
_____
_____
_____
_____
_____
_____

Literary Form

_____
_____
_____
_____
_____
_____

Scripture 3

Who

_____
_____
_____
_____
_____
_____
_____

What

_____
_____
_____
_____
_____
_____
_____

Where

_____
_____
_____
_____
_____
_____
_____

When

_____
_____
_____
_____
_____
_____
_____

Literary Form

_____
_____
_____
_____
_____
_____
_____

CHAPTER 6

HOMILETICS AND HOMILETICAL STRUCTURE

We are going to do it! We are going to build a sermon. We have now done the work of exegesis and hermeneutics. We have done our best to understand and internalize the Scriptures. We have anticipation and excitement as we think about how to best present what God has taught us. As the little cursor blinks on an open page, we are excited to get something on the computer screen. This may feel like that moment in a TV show where the scene cuts and the credits roll, and you have to wait till next week to see what happens. So, for that, I apologize. But before we move any further, I want to give you my philosophy when it comes to Homiletics which, again, means the art of preaching.

Philosophy of Homiletics

My homiletical philosophy is simple. I want to you to learn how to be the unique artist and communicator that God created you to be. I came to this passion for two reasons:

1. *You are unique.* The Artist of all artists, God himself, painted you and each stroke was unique and genius. He gives every preacher characteristics that are unlike any other and a backstory that can be compared but not matched. Each preacher comes with unique pains and joys. Each preacher has a carefully crafted personality that will (and needs to) come through in their preaching if he or she will let it. The brilliance of the vastness and diversity of God's universe is illustrated in the great diversity of those He calls and equips to preach. We all have different tendencies, desires, upbringings and triggers. Your intricate DNA string represents the creativity of God. God didn't want you to abandon that creativity when you took up preaching. He doesn't desire you to leave your fingerprint behind when crafting a sermon. He wants you to be all of who he has created you to be when you stand before other disciples who are learning to be all of who they are for God's glory and the sake of the Gospel. Will you be an artist who trusts that the Great Artist painted you with intense purpose and not wild flippancy?

Now, I will admit that I believe on average it takes about 250 sermons for a preacher to really be comfortable in their own skin. Said another way, it takes about 5 years of consistent weekly preaching for a preacher to find their own voice and become comfortable with that voice. Furthermore, I don't think it helps that most of the preaching books on the market come with a strict structure and a weighty checklist. While I honor them and while they pave the way for other preaching books, they have discipled us all in predictability. To preach "right" we will stick to the structure and be careful to let our personality really come out from behind that podium. Again, as mentioned in Chapter 1, every good scientist has some art in their craft and every good artist attains a science that really helps their art thrive. I think that we have done a full court press on the Science of preaching. Because of that, it takes longer to learn how to be yourself in the pulpit. It takes a while to know your rhythm, know where God's power is in you, and know how to build practices that carry you through the marathon of consistent preaching. Honestly, it takes a while to escape the cage of the particular preaching method we were taught in college or seminary.

2. *Because you are unique, the structure and rhythm that you settle into will be unique.* There are a plethora of sermon structures and different ways to get your sermon from paper to delivery. Here are a few simple sermon structures just to get the ball rolling:

Narrative- A sermon structure which uses biblical and human stories as an outline to get to the principal truth.

Topical- A sermon structure which explains a biblical view on a theological or relevant human topic.

Expository- A sermon structure which gives a comprehensive explanation of a particular Scripture in context.

Recently, Dr. Eric Mason (founder and pastor of Epiphany Fellowship in Philadelphia, PA) categorized some other sermon structures in a Twitter post. I will place them in my own words but credit his unique take on the categories.

Topical expository- This is obviously a combination of expository and topical. The main difference here is that there is a clear exegesis of the Scriptures used and the Scriptures clearly take center stage. In contrast, in some topical structures, it may seem that the Scriptures were a sprinkling in or used as a jumping off point for the message.

Doctrinal Exposition- A comprehensive view from the Scriptures on a doctrinal topic.

Felt Need Exposition- A comprehensive view from the Scriptures on a felt need topic.

Current Event Exposition- A comprehensive view from the Scriptures on a tension we face today.

Book Exposition- A verse by verse study through a book of the Bible.

There are other forms and structures to sermon building and you will undoubtedly develop a favorite. You will need to push yourself to have other structures, but in your unique skin, you will likely feel compelled toward a few structures.

There are also different ways to develop a finished product from pen to paper and from paper to delivery. Here are a few ways:

Manuscript- Some preachers prefer to write out every single word. They will craft up to eight pages line by line, word by word. I recommend doing this for your first 50 sermons. Writing out every word will teach you a lot about yourself. It will reveal habits and will keep your craft tight. It will push you in ways that outlining cannot push you. It also forces you to really learn to craft compelling language and important sentences. As we get into the homiletical components, you will learn principles and practices for writing an effective manuscript. One of those practices will be the importance of certain sentences in your sermon. When you manuscript, you are forced to take care of each sentence in a way that builds your language ability.

Outline- Some preachers prefer to preach from an outline. They type or write out their most important bullet points and ideas. For them, less is more.

Combination- Some preachers prefer a combination of a manuscript and an outline, putting a little more meat on certain sections.

Unicorn- Some preachers are unicorns. They put a few marks in their Bibles, draw a bunch of lines from one Scripture to the next, color in a picture of a cross in their journal and deliver a masterful sermon.

Whoever you are, God created you to be you. You are uniquely made, uniquely gifted and He expects who you are to be a part of your sermon—construction and delivery. He wants you to settle into what excites you and brings you joy. Just like a marathon, if you don't learn to love the process of running and if you don't learn what rhythm works for you in preparation, you won't be a marathon runner. It is that simple. Structures and homiletical philosophies that choke out your artistic mojo can be detrimental to your joy and to the longevity of your preaching. So, how will we put this homiletical philosophy into practice?

You have the ingredients; let's cook!

Anne can cook anything. I mean anything. I am a blessed man and I know it. Early on in marriage that blessing went straight to my gut. She would make me sandwiches that made all the husbands jealous. I loved it... a little too much. Because she is 1st generation Filipino-American, she grew up around Filipino cuisine and so when she married me, she learned how to cook all sorts of Italian dishes and American fare. She did this because she loved me and because Filipino food takes forever! She learned how to cook Korean dishes, which is probably our favorite corner of the earth when it comes to cuisine, and she has made really complicated dishes. Have I said how much I love her yet? For some reason though, she cannot assemble the two things that I can assemble. I assemble; I don't cook. My two areas of expertise are the bagel with cream cheese and the bowl of cereal. I lived on these two culinary creations from ages 3 to 23. Anne just does not get it. When making a bowl of cereal, she puts the milk in first! You read that correctly. What kind of monster puts the milk in first? When assembling a bagel, you receive the bagel and think, "where is all the cream cheese"? I mean I am a New York/New Jersey guy at heart which means cream cheese should be spilling out over the edge. I say all this to make you hungry and to make the point that cooking is not just about a strict recipe. Cooking is about measurement, timing and feeling. Anne clearly does not put the same feelings into a bowl of cereal that she does a good steak alfredo. The nerve of her.

In the previous chapters, my goal has been to give you the necessary ingredients and a semblance of a recipe to go by. Now, I want you to cook. You will make mistakes and you will get frustrated. You will pour too much of this in and add too much of that. You will learn every time. And in the end, you will learn how to be yourself and you will learn exactly what type of preacher you were called to be. Philosophy makes sense before structure. Now, let's move into your homiletical structure.

Homiletical Structure

Before we move into building your homiletical structure or outline, I want to take you deep into the bowels of one of Americas favorite pastimes…Whack-a-Mole. It may have been a while since you have had a really good bout with whacking a mole, so let me remind you of the setting. This game is usually played in a children's pizza, arcade and recreational center. These are the establishments I do everything to avoid, but somehow end up at four times a year. There are only a few games that rescue this hellscape for me. One is the mini basketball game. I try to motivate one of my kids in that direction every time we are there. Unfortunately, my non-athletic wife beat me 47-24 once, and my pride has yet to rehabilitate. The only other game left is Whack-a-Mole. There is nothing that gets the heart racing quite like Whack-a-Mole. Whack-a-Mole is 40 seconds of unhindered attention. It is like gathering your brain cells into a football huddle and saying, "Ok, we are going to need everyone on this play." The key to Whack-a-Mole is *central* focus and *peripheral* focus. You have a mini, cushioned hammer in your hand, and little laughing moles are popping up from out of focus and in focus. You don't have time to tilt your head and eyes to every corner of the Whack-a-Mole universe. You need to keep your eyes and head on a central location while also keeping your eyes on the peripheral. It is a lot like when your mom told you, "I am going to keep an eye on you". That did not mean that she was going to stare at you with both eyes the entire time. That meant that she was going to have a peripheral view of you. It meant at times she would have a central view, but if she didn't have a central view, she would keep a peripheral view. If you want to be invited onto the professional Whack-a-Mole circuit, you will have to practice those very same fundamentals. You must always have a central view, but always keep an eye on the peripheral.

Like Whack-a-Mole, your preaching has both core components and peripheral components. Core components are central and fundamental components that must be a part of every sermon. Peripheral components are components that you must keep a peripheral eye on as you build your sermon—they aren't central, but essential.

The Bridge

You have arrived at The Bridge (see image). On one side of the bridge is all of your exegetical work. On the other side of The Bridge is your homiletical structure. Some of the work you did is going to make it across that bridge right into your structure and sermon. Some of it will not make the journey. Three quick principles as you start to decide what makes it across the bridge:

1. Hermeneutics is for culture, not just the Scriptures- Remember, hermeneutics is a hovering idea, flying down and inserting itself in many parts of your sermon-building process. Hermeneutical principles can be applied to Scripture and culture. On this bridge you are applying good hermeneutics not just to the Scriptures, but to the people that you are preaching to. It is time, because you gave the Scriptures proper shrift, to think about how to apply it to your context, culture, and your moment in time. Good preachers apply a sound hermeneutic to both.

2. The Gate Principle- The Gate Principle is as follows: It is easier to keep something out than kick something out. This bridge needs to have a tight gate. A gate made of iron that rivals a stingy country. Once you get an idea of something that you want to be in your sermon, and you hang onto it, whether it fits cleanly in the flow of your sermon or not, it is hard to get out. We have all seen preacher after preacher allow a story into their sermon that had no business being there. Or maybe they hung onto a historical context nugget that was so nerdy and intriguing, they just had to keep it in. It turns out, it was only interesting to them. Tighten up the gate my friends!

3. The Shrink Principle- The Shrink Principle is as follows: The goal of preaching is not to say a lot of nothing, but to say the perfect amount of something. The Shrink principle is best buddies with The Gate Principle. I like to picture the two principles sharing a pour-over at the local, overpriced coffee shop. Be careful what crosses this bridge. You will want to learn how to get good at turning paragraphs into clean one-liners, not clean one-liners into bloated paragraphs with confusing facts. Twitter has a complicated history and all of its effects on society are yet to be revealed, but it did teach us one thing; shrinking language is good. Using fewer characters forces us to be masters of language and profound communicators. At the mouth of this bridge, think shrink, not bloat.

Core Components

Now that we understand the bridge, let's bring more defined lines to what constitutes a *core component*. A core component is a critical and central component of your sermon. It is a must have—a thing the sermon needs in order to function properly and effectively. There are wants and needs in life. I want a Tesla, but it is hard for me to make the case that a Tesla fits in my personal need category. There is no judgment on Tesla owners here, just a self-awareness that my Honda will do just fine. However, I do need oxygen. The core components fit in the need category when it comes to your sermon. They will be the main organs of your sermon, pumping blood and oxygen to the rest of the body and the limbs of your message. They are your *Core*

Components.

Principal Truth

Principal Truth- The main truth the text is communicating.

If core components are your main organs, then the *Principal Truth* is your heart. It is the organ that pumps blood to the rest of the body of your sermon. Quite intentionally, it will be connected to almost everything in your sermon and everything will be connected to it. You discovered through exegesis and hermeneutics what the Principal Truth was. You discovered what you believe is the authors foundational proposition. Other books have called it the "big idea" or the "main idea". Haddon Robinson, who may be the first to call it the big idea in his book *Biblical Preaching* talks about it in a very targeted manner: "*A sermon should be a bullet, not a buckshot. Ideally each sermon is the explanation, interpretation, or application of a single dominant idea supported by other ideas, all drawn from one passage or several passages of Scripture.*"[14]

In other words, the human mind can't handle your spray of thought bullets. Just because your mind can grasp your specific brand of tornado reasoning, it doesn't mean your people can. The Holy Spirit, through the author in their original context, did the work to find and communicate a Principal Truth. It is both helpful to the preacher and helpful to the audience not just to find that truth but to communicate it with precision.

Broad View of your Principal Truth

Let me give you a broad view of the position of your Principal Truth and then a more precise view. In the broadest sense, you will build up to your Principal Truth (inductive reasoning) and then break it down (deductive reasoning) (see the graph). Like a good story, you will create some form of tension leading up to the Principal Truth. The Principal Truth will be the climax of the story and then the rest of the sermon will be an unraveling of that truth.

Let me pause here and remind you that sermon building is an art. The question you undoubtedly want to ask here, is, "Should the Principal Truth go at the beginning or the end?" Every story is different. Every teacher/preacher is different. Some preachers are highly inductive and love

---

[14] Robinson, H. W. *Biblical preaching: The development and delivery of expository messages.* Baker Academic, a division of Baker Publishing Group, 2014, pp35.

the tension. They spend much of their sermons creating wonder and conviction, giving the listener ample time to thirst for the main truth that will blindside them without a moment's notice. Other preachers are a lot like Paul in their communication. They state the Principal Truth right up front and then unravel it through reasoning. They state some connecting truths, and then explain the Principal Truth in great detail. I believe it is wisdom to take each text and Principal Truth and let it dictate the flow of your structure. It is wisdom to sit in a quiet place with the Spirit and let the supernatural take place. The Holy Spirit wants to be involved in the beginning of your sermon building, not just the desperate delivery. Because of that, you will have new inspiration and new prophetic imagination every time you sit down with a new text in a sacred space. Let the text you are preaching and the Spirit who is illuminating the text and empowering your preaching to drive the sermon's flow.

Precise View of your Principal Truth

The clearest sermon structures are those that have a clear, compelling and connected Principal Truth. The actual statement is clear and lacks confusion. It is compelling and punchy. It hits people in their gut. The concentration here is not that your statement has flash, but that it is faithful, honest and driven by the Scriptures. That will make your statement compelling. It is both connected to the Scriptures and connected to the other core components of your sermon structure. I have worded the components in this way not because I want to reinvent the wheel or try to be cute, but because I hope to bring clarity to your Principal Truth. If there is to be clarity, there should be a tight tether from the Principal Truth to the Principal Problem you are addressing and the Principal Question you are asking.

I know I have just introduced two new sermonic components—the Principal Problem and the Principal Question; these need a bit of definition before we move forward. The Principal Problem is the main problem addressed by the text regarding the human condition. The Principal Question is the main question of the soul that is connected to the text and the human condition. In other words, how do the Scriptures answer the deepest and most pressing questions of our souls? To help illustrate the connection between these essential parts of the sermon I will build a bare-bones sermon structure so that you can see this connectedness in action. We will use the Scripture to highlight core and peripheral components as we continue through our process. I chose an Old Testament text because they are often a bit trickier when trying to obtain the Principal Truth.

Jonah 4:1-11(ESV)

"But it displeased Jonah exceedingly, and he was angry. And he prayed to the Lord and said, 'OLord, is not this what I said when I was yet in my country? That is why I made haste to flee to Tarshish; for I knew that you are a gracious God and merciful, slow to anger and abounding in steadfast love, and relenting from disaster. Therefore now, O Lord, please take my life from me, for it is better for me to die than to live.' And the Lord said, 'Do you do well to be angry?' Jonah went out of the city and sat to the east of the city and made a booth for himself there. He sat under it in the shade, till he should see what would become of the city. Now the Lord God appointed a plant and made it come up over Jonah, that it might be a shade over his head, to save him from his discomfort. So Jonah was exceedingly glad because of the plant. But when dawn came up the next day, God appointed a worm that attacked the plant, so that it withered. When the sun rose, God appointed a scorching east wind, and the sun beat down on the head of Jonah so that he was faint. And he asked that he might die and said, 'It is better for me to die than to live.' But God said to Jonah, 'Do you do well to be angry for the plant?' And he said, 'Yes, I do well to be angry, angry enough to die.' And the Lord said, 'You pity the plant, for which you did not labor, nor did you make it grow, which came into being in a night and perished in a night. And should not I pity Nineveh, that great city, in which there are more than 120,000 persons who do not know their right hand from their left, and also much cattle?'"

Principal Truth
God is a God of your insides and intentions, not your outsides and outcomes.

How I arrived here:
The work of Exegesis and Hermeneutics led me to a man who had a large platform and calling. He goes into one of the most dangerous and vile cities in the world. The King who is most likely King Shalmaneser III is a plundering and powerful king who was famous for conquering the Babylonians, Mesopotamians, and the Syrians. That's an impressive rap sheet. It is also an intimidating one. The fact that Jonah would speak and a whole country including their king would turn to God, is quite literally the biggest win on anyone's ministry resume. That is legacy building and the outcome of that ministry event and the measurables on the outsides will land you in the canon of Scripture. However, Jonah's insides are rotten according to Jonah 4:1, 5 and 9-11. His intentions and insides are rotten even though his outside outcomes are legacy building. God is not pleased.

Principal truths on the Principal Truth
1. Mirror the heart- Notice that the Principal Truth can, at times, come off as a summary. However, the goal is not to summarize the passage but to mirror the author's heart, in context, in a clear, compelling and connected manner. All of your exegetical and hermeneutical work has a goal. The goal is to attempt to figure out what the author is saying, crossing the cultural bridge, and stating a Principal Truth to your audience.

2. Compress and rework the language- Remember, if I am using *the Gate Principle* and *the Shrink Principle*, the goal is not to say everything or to allow every good thought into my outline. I want to say the most with the least. I want to capture the heart of the text in a concise manner. This takes some time to rework and compress these sentences. Don't be surprised if this takes you 5 to 55 tries. You will get better at it as you go along.

3. The Scriptures are alive- Often, if you are doing this in a cohort or classroom setting, you will find that your Principal Truths are not always the same. Every once in a while, if you teach a text one year and then teach it again in a year or two, your Principal Truths may sound different! Don't stress out; you are not a heretic. Remember that the Scriptures are alive and hit people differently. They breathe differently inside of you and although the author and contexts have not changed, God's illumination of the text can hit you and a group of people from different angles. You are also at a different place in your sanctification process than you were a year ago. Your spiritual goggles have more precision and your life experiences have led you to a more mature faith. This is part of the process of interpretation. Your hermeneutics will mature, and your spiritual senses will heighten as you grow in Christ. This will lead to an ever-growing illumination.

4. This is your heart, so make sure it's healthy- Some of the most shocking deaths around us are the deaths of people who look healthy. They are young and fit. Everything on their body may be healthy, but the organ that feeds all the other organs is not and they have a heart attack. It does not matter how great the bicep looks or if they never smoked and have good lungs. If the main mechanism pumping to all the other mechanisms is not healthy, the whole body is not healthy. Take care of this Principal Truth! Everything should be connected to it in some way shape or form. This may determine if you are both faithful to the text and faithful to clarity. No pressure!

Principal Problem

Now that you have targeted the Principal Truth, you can build your other components off of it. The heart can pump blood to the other parts of the body. The Principal Truth is the first of these three main components. The next two, the Principal Problem and The Principal Question, build off of the first. To have a really clean and simple outline, you will want to tether to all three together. You can tether them together in language. You can use similar wording and, put simply, you can use one to build the other.

Principal Truth
God is a God of your insides and intentions, not your outsides and outcomes.
Principal Problem
God desires to work through us and around us, but until we let him address our inside intentions, our outside outcomes won't matter.

How I arrived here:
I used the Principal Truth as a launch pad and made sure I stayed close to it in phrasing and language. Since my Principal Truth comes from the text, it is easy to make the connection back and keep the two connected. Jonah's inside intentions come from anger, judgement, self-righteousness and selfishness. Because of that, his outside outcomes are not working out for him and will leave him with a legacy he probably doesn't want. God is still faithful to Nineveh and to Jonah in the end, but God is also going to address Jonah's inside intentions.

Broad View of the Principal Problem
The Principal Problem, in its most basic sense, is intended to create tension in the hearer and a need for the Gospel. It is hard to grow outside of humility. It is hard to learn without a learning posture. It often helps the hearer when the preacher brings awareness to a sinful state or a broken tendency coming from the Scriptures. A clear picture of this is during Peter's epic, mega church in a day sermon in Acts 2. He looks at them and tells them in a few words that they have royally screwed up and killed the Savior of the world. It doesn't really get worse than that. In this moment, he is making them aware of the Principal Problem. It is an easy argument to say that "You killed Jesus" is the most effective Principal Problem ever. Their response is telling and profound. *"Now when they heard this they were cut to the heart, and said to Peter and the rest of the apostles, 'Brothers, what shall we do?"* (Acts 2:37). That phrase "cut to the heart" is the Greek word, *katanyssomai,* which means to prick and agitate vehemently. This is the appropriate feeling. The appropriate feeling also leads to an appropriate response. "Brothers, what shall we do?" The Principal Problem created tension and need for the Gospel. They became aware of their sin and repentance, and a turning to Jesus became possible.

The Bible talks a lot about sin and so should we. The Father addresses what exists inside of His children that could cause them harm, and so should the preacher. We call it the Principal Problem because there isn't always a blatant sin that the Scriptures are addressing. There is, however, always a problem with the human condition based on the truth that is being presented in a text of Scripture. There is an opposite of the truth and there is something relevant in every text that will draw focus to the sin crouching at our door.

83

Let me offer a more precise view in the form of specific possibilities of Principal Problems.

Possibilities of the Principal Problem

1. Sins of Omission- *Something I should have done but did not do.* God gave me faithful clarity and I ignored it. He told me through the Scriptures, a prompt of the Spirit, or others what obedience looked like, and I omitted it.

2. Sins of Commission- *Something I should not have done but did anyway.* God was clear on what would be harmful to myself and those around me. He was clear on what is against His law of love, but I did not obey His command and chose selfishness over Him.

3. Individual Sin- Sins of omission and commission can be talked about on different levels as well. You can choose to talk about the sin of the individual that is clear in that Scripture. You can talk about how that fallen condition plays out in an individual context. I encourage you to refer back to our section on "cultivating authenticity", and maybe see this as an opportunity to talk about your own individual sin. It would help if we started to break down the culture of leader idolization. We find it easy to blame the follower when a leader is lifted too high, but it is often a case where the leader never confesses a sin or fallen condition.

4. Institutional Sin- There are patterns that this institution of the Church needs to address. There is a way that the Bride has sinned against the Bridegroom. Corporate confession brings entire nations to turn toward God in the Old Testament and New Testament. See Jonah, Nehemiah and Acts 2 as good examples. I have seen corporate confession start mini revivals in my own denomination.

5. Interpersonal Sin- Jesus gave us two laws to fulfill the whole law and one of them was to love our neighbor as ourselves. There is always interpersonal sin that could be pointed out.

6. Other- There is always an option of "other" on surveys and interest forms. This is because most things don't nestle into a black or white category. The same goes for the text. There may not be a glaring sin popping out of the text, but there will be a human pattern or a form of brokenness that presents itself. Pull it out, match the language to your Principal Truth and start heading in the direction of your Principal Question.

Principal Question

Preaching is not just about the proclamation of the preacher but about the ownership of the listener. Most of what you have said already has come from your work and wrestle with the text. The Principal Question will take the wrestling match to the ring of the listener's soul. They will have to dig down into their heart or the central thought seat and answer this question for themselves. If you build ownership into your preaching, you may just start to build a culture of ownership. If people start to answer questions for themselves in relationship with God, that may build ownership into their intimacy with Jesus and eventually ownership regarding the mission of God for their lives. In other words, ownership driven preaching leads to ownership of intimacy and ownership of discipleship and mission. I can't think of a much more important culture to build amongst the family to whom you are preaching, and the Principal Question is a great way build ownership into your preaching.

Here is what I came up with for this sermon:
Principal Truth
God is a God of your insides and intentions, not your outsides and outcomes.
Principal Problem
God desires to work through us and around us, but until we let him address our inside intentions, our outside outcomes won't matter.
Principal Question
Everyone has collective mission they are called to. That is, something God has called us all to take part in. Everyone also has selective mission. That is, something specific and relevant to you right now. Something God has selected you for! What is that selective calling and what do your insides look like as you step into that calling? Do you have good motives and intentions, or do you have similar insides to Jonah?

How I arrived here:
The Principal Truth and Principal Problem were both hovering in the macro. They were broad sweeping and weren't sniping the individual conscience. The Principal Question, therefore, can play that role in this circumstance. I want the audience to be deeply introspective as well as find a desire to answer that Principal Question. It also comes straight from my Principal Truth and Principal Problem, so they are connected in language and idea. Because they are interconnected, that helps me stay close to the Scripture.

Broad View of the Principal Question
Jesus asked questions so loaded they looked like your high school car when you were on the way to buy lunch. He looks at His disciples at one point and asks, "Who do you say I am?" That's the type of question that will

make you feel like you swallowed a rock while trying to answer it. Jesus asked a lifelong paralytic, "Do you want to be healed?" How about when Adam and Eve have just sinned and Adam knows that God knows his exact location, but asks anyway, "Adam, where are you?" Jesus has answered questions with questions. "Whose face is on that coin?" God does this throughout the Scriptures for many reasons, but one of the main reasons is because He wants the listener to stop renting someone else's ideas of God. He wants them to answer the question for themselves and purchase the truth for their own soul. Questions always lead to wrestling and wrestling leads to honest reflection. This is why the Principal Question is a core component of your sermon. By the end of the sermon, you will have given them a question they must answer. You will rarely answer the question in a comprehensive way, but hopefully you give them the tools to wrestle with God. Hopefully, when the dust settles, they will have gained ownership over their own relationship with God and the implications of the Scriptures.

Some Additive Truths About the Principal Question

1. The art of asking the Question- While the Principal Question should be just that, the main or primary question connected to your Principal Truth, you can bring the art of questioning into other parts of your sermon. Again, questions create tension and ownership, so carefully placed questions throughout your sermon will prick the conscience in the right ways. However, I would caution against asking a slew of questions that you don't intend to help your audience to answer.

2. Where does it go?- It is usually this moment in coaching where the order question is asked. Does the Principal Question have to come *after* the Principal Problem? Do these three core components need to go in sequence—Truth, Problem, then Question? It is also at this time that I like to remind folks that Homiletics is *the art of preaching.* At a core value level, this process is designed to give you core and peripheral elements and let you paint. Sit down with the Holy Spirit and the text and pray. Let your imagination paint a picture; let it help you tell the story. Sometimes that story will ask a question right at the top. It will create a deep tension and a quiet moment in the room, and that will provide you the opportunity to maximize that tension. The critical point here is that you identify what these components are and how they are connected!

3. Answer the question yourself!- Your own ownership over this question will bring power and authenticity to your sermon. It will bring your emotion and connection to the text and your people to the forefront. It will pull your posture out from behind the pulpit to stand directly in front of the people. They will be able to see what Jesus is doing in your life, or what you haven't

addressed yet, and it will inspire them to be authentic Jesus followers. I can't think of a more important mission in sermon prep.

Connecting Truths

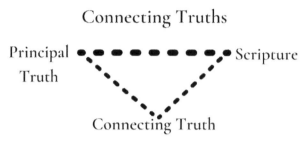

Connecting Truths are supporting truths that connect to your Principal Truth and to the text. Like the Principal Truth, Connecting Truths are also *anchored* in the Scripture, a component that will be explained later. There are a few options here for you to choose what your Connecting Truths will look like. You can divide up your Principal Truth into pieces or if the Scripture dictates, you can state other truths that fit under the umbrella of your Principal Truth. You can also choose to state other truths that connect only to the Text and not to the Principal Truth. This is not an unfaithful endeavor; it may just lack clarity because it only has one anchor and not two. If you build your sermon so that each truth not only has a direct line to the Text but also a direct line to the Principal Truth, it is a safer bet that you will have clear navigation throughout your sermon.

I will demonstrate some connecting truths and the rest of the Core Components through a different sermon that a homiletics class and I worked on together. God is speaking a very similar Principal Truth as we saw in our Jonah passage. Let's take a look and see if we can trace the Scriptural connect between Old and New Testament that shows God's heart for his people.

Mark 12:41-44(ESV)
"And he sat down opposite the treasury and watched the people putting money into the offering box. Many rich people put in large sums. And a poor widow came and put in two small copper coins, which make a penny. And he called his disciples to him and said to them, 'Truly, I say to you, this poor widow has put in more than all those who are contributing to the offering box. For they all contributed out of their abundance, but she

out of her poverty has put in everything she had, all she had to live on."

Principal Truth
When giving, Jesus cares more about the motive of your heart, than the measure in your hand.
Principal Problem
We tend to give from the motives of performance and religious reward rather than faith and worship.
Principal Question
What are the motives of your heart when you are giving to Jesus and His mission?
Connecting Truths
Good Motives
1. Faith
2. Worship
Bad Motives
1. Performance
2. Religious Reward

How I arrived here:

You will notice that these Connecting Truths have multiple anchors. They are anchored to the Principal Truth in that they are motives of the heart. The Connecting Truths are also anchored to the Scriptural narrative. The temple in Jesus' time was riddled with notorious performance-based religious practices from the Pharisees and upper echelon of temple attendees. We will preach with enhanced clarity when we anchor the Connecting Truths to both the Principal Truth of the text and the Scriptural narrative. It will lead to a clearer message because my connecting truths are connected closely to text and Principal Truth. As long as I don't wander too far from the Principal Truth or forget to practice the *Gate Principal* or the *Shrink Principal*, preaching the Connecting Truths will bring clarity to our preaching. And it will help us produce a pretty tight, bare bones outline to build off of.

If I may make a suggestion, for the first 50-100 sermons, build your outline first. Practicing faithful exegesis and applying a sound hermeneutic while building a clear outline may seem annoying at first. It may seem time consuming and cumbersome to put in all this work.

In any sport, mechanics seem daunting and annoying at times. The discipline in baseball to keep your shoulder up, head down and back foot planted seems like torture when you just want to naturally thrust your whole body through the ball and knock it over the fence. In golf, you would probably just rather "Happy Gilmore" the ball 400 hundred miles instead of practicing proper form and discipline. In weightlifting, I can promise a pulled muscle or 12 if you go for big weight and no form. It will be the same with your sermon building. At this point, let me remind you that order matters. Good sermons demand that we practice proper form and stay close to the Scriptures. You will eventually develop good muscles and reflexes. It might be annoying, but faithful and clear sermons come through perseverance.

Application
How does this truth apply?

Now that we have a basic outline, it's time to move on to some other core components that will highlight these truths we've already discovered. These components will color in the lines that you have previously drawn. *Application* is a simple way to color in in the picture that those lines create.

This is the time in the sermon when you answer the question, "How does this truth apply?" You have stated a Truth, a Connecting Truth or a Principal Problem. Now we can apply those truths to ourselves and our listeners in a personal and relevant way.

An application can fit in micro and macro categories. How does it apply to the individual, or the institution of Church? How did it apply to the moment in Ancient Rome or how does it apply in modern Toledo, OH? The application can be a short paragraph or an entire page. There is a lot of freedom in application. The lanes of the highway are kind of endless. If you can't tell by now, I like structure—enough to give guardrails and direction but not so much as to suffocate or stifle creativity.

Here are some *guard rails* of application that you should think through.
Guard Rail 1- Think cul-de-sacs, not trips through the woods. Flying over this guard rail is really easy for both newer and older preachers. Applications are meant to be cul-de-sacs. Meaning they are not meant to be long and meandering detours. Application is taking a quick trip down a street, round the cul-de-sac, and then right back onto the main road. The main road is the truth that you are trying to convey. The temptation is to like this application so much that you end up expanding on it and introducing a whole new set of truths that may or may not be connected to your Principal Truth. Sooner or later, those truths are not Connected Truths. They are not connected to the text, your outline, or even the previous truth. Have you ever been in the woods and realized you are going in circles? Welcome to the feeling of your audience. They don't know where you are and how you got there. You have abandoned clarity. Make your application and then tie it back to where you came from. Come back to the main road.

Guard Rail 2- Make sure it applies! I know this seems really obvious and maybe even patronizing. But it is a good question to ask of your applications. Does this apply to the listener? Is this relevant to them, the condition of their soul and what they are going through. Maybe up to this point in your preaching career, you have preached theoretical sermons filled with ethereal ideas and grand philosophies. These kinds of sermons float above the heads of your listeners and don't penetrate into their hearts. Like the Principal Question, this is a component meant to get inside the listener's story. It is meant to work its way into their house. Application isn't just a theological idea. It's not a proposal or concept that intrigues you in some way, shape or form. It must apply to them personally. And if it applies to them personally…how?

Illustration

How will you illustrate this truth?

Jesus mainly taught in narrative form. He taught with pictures and stories. He preached the most important sermons of all time using pictures of birds, farmers and sheep. He taught using illustrations that His listeners could touch, see, and feel. He used people as examples, and he exemplified the Kingdom to people with illustration. By teaching this way, Jesus shows us that preaching is about the heart. He wanted to connect to the human heart, and the best way to do that is through illustration. It is critical that you work story and a diverse palette of illustrations into your preaching. Some argue that illustration and story are not core components of the sermon—as long as information is disseminated, the sermon has served its purpose. To those who might think that stories lack the theological heft to communicate heavy duty theological concepts; to those who think verse-by-verse exposition is all we need—to those I'd simply point them to the teachings of Jesus and Paul. They both used story and illustration to connect people to the God who loves them with a reckless, relentless, and pursuant love.

Here is a catalogue of Story and Illustrative options:

Personal Story- For many preachers, there is an invisible wall between the pulpit and their audience. It's a wall of protection. It allows the preacher to deliver a distant monologue. It hides them and keeps them from being seen by the people to whom they preach. This wall hides the faults and foibles of the pastor, but it also shields the people from the work Christ is doing in the heart of their pastor.

Vulnerability is one of the most powerful tools God uses to connect the preacher to his or her people. Personal stories are some of the most powerful illustrations we have in our arsenal. By sharing your triumphs and your failures you show the work of Holy Spirit in your own life. It is a great way for you to feel the truth and allow others to see it in your life. It is a great way for you stop preaching *at* folks and start preaching *with* them. Your involvement and ownership over this in your own life will do wonders for your message.

Hint: Too many personal stories in a sermon can make the sermon seem self-centered and self-serving. Also, if you are the hero of every story and Jesus is not, then you will be the hero in your audience's mind, and I am sure that does not connect back to the Scriptures.

Human Story- Human story is a story about another person—either current or historical. You could have a personal relationship with the person or not. Human stories of brokenness, faith and mission can be really impactful. Biographies are popular because God made people fascinating. He made us a beautiful mess complete with drama and triumph.

Hint: Get someone's permission if you are going to share their story. You never want to embarrass anyone or share someone else's dirty laundry. This is also not a moment to rebuke someone publicly.

Creation Illustration- The elements contained in creation reveal the Creator. How and what God created go hand in hand with His personality, creativity, and greatness. The glory and wonder of God's creation are unfathomable and there is new revelation every day, even for the unbeliever, when they take a moment to pause and look at creation. Jesus often preached from creation; how a tree grew or what a season produced. I don't think I am going too far out on a limb here when I say if someone wanted to take on the challenge, they could use an illustration from something in creation all 52 weeks out of the year. I don't recommend it, but that limb won't crack.

Object Illustration- Take an object of any kind and use the makeup of it or the functionality of it and use that as an illustration. If a creation illustration is telling a story from creation, then an object illustration is telling a story from some part of creation. Jesus had a great object illustration:

"Why do you see the speck that is in your brother's eye, but do not notice the log that is in your own eye? Or how can you say to your brother, 'Let me take the speck out of your eye,' when there is the log in your own eye? You hypocrite, first take the log out of your own eye, and then you will see clearly to take the speck out of your brother's eye." (Matthew 7: 3-5, ESV).

How many preachers have meandered up to the pulpit carrying a "plank" they bought from Home Depot?

Hint: If at all possible, have the object with you. We are visual creatures, are we not?

Seinfeld Illustration- For years, I could not categorize this one. A preacher would be up there, and I really liked this method of illustration and this approach of drawing me to a truth. But for the life of me, I could not put it into a nice, neat category until a watched episodes of one of the greatest sitcoms of all time…Seinfeld. Seinfeld, for the young folks in the back, was, by its own admission, a sitcom about nothing. The creators and writers of Seinfeld did an amazing job of taking the everyday mundane activities and making a big deal out of them. It was a gift. They would turn the normal, like adopting a one mile stretch of highway or taking aluminum cans to be recycled, into a big, dramatic and funny story. Some of you will be really gifted at taking the everyday mundane tasks, like checking in at the airport, to illustrate the truth you're trying to communicate.

Cultural Trend Illustration- Culture is a violent river we aimlessly float down whether we know it or not. There are cultural trends in the Church and worldly trends that are relevant to us today. They are often contradictory to the Kingdom or at least tell us how our kingdoms are colliding. Right or wrong, cultural trends can be very effective illustrations for your preaching.

Biblical and Historical Context Illustration- The cultural and contextual nuances of the Scriptures can be fascinating. If you are like me, you have found that people are generally quite nerdy. The way the games in Greece highlight Paul's teaching in 1 Corinthians 9, or the way the water distribution around Laodicea illustrated what Jesus, through John, meant by "lukewarm" in Revelation 3 generally will draw people in. Not only does it stir up fascination, but it drops you on the sand of an ancient city. You can feel, see and picture the context of the Scriptures in new and exciting ways. I think my favorite sermon series of all time was preaching through the seven letters of Revelation. Each time Jesus spoke to a new Church, I got to do a deep dive into the particular historical context of the city He was addressing.

Biblical Story- The Bible is an amazing piece of literature. A divinely inspired collection of 66 books crossing thousands of years and dozens of authors. It tells dramatic, devastating and miraculous stories. All of those stories connect to the same God and run congruent with His larger story. The grand story has everything you could want in a story. It has an epic arc, a villain and a hero. Each story contained in the Bible also has the core elements of a good story. It can be really helpful to also prove the consistency of the character of God by illustrating your truth with a story from the Scriptures.

Hint: Too many Bible stories in one sermon can become confusing to you or your audience. Because the Bible is so jam-packed with eternal truth it is quite easy to go off into the woods during a biblical narrative and lose the truth you were trying to illustrate.

More Helpful Hints:

1. Help! I can't find an illustration! We have all been there. We know that the truth that we are on absolutely needs an illustration. It is a really good point, important to the structure of your sermon, and it simply needs to be illustrated! I have found it helpful to shrink what you are trying to say into a sentence. Go back to the Principal Truth or the Connecting Truth that you are trying to communicate and shrink what you are trying to say through your illustration into a clear and concise sentence. Say that sentence over and over again. Repeat that sentence like a weirdo in your office or study until it sparks something. Walk around if you need to. Don't give up, it will come.

2. Hit your sweet spot but diversify your portfolio. We are all aware of the folks who only use one kind of illustration. That may be nice for a sermon or 12. However, by sermon 13 or so, the people are screaming for you to try a different kind of illustration. Yes, it is great that you have a sweet spot or a certain type of illustration that you are good at and comfortable with, but if you are going to keep a crowd with you week after week, you need to diversify your portfolio.

3. Repeat that sentence. Hey, remember that sentence from helpful hint #1? That sentence you crafted so that it would be helpful for you to find clarity and options in what you are illustrating? If it is really a concise and compelling sentence, repeat it over and over throughout your illustration. Repetition is so, so good! And repeating that sentence over and over again will help you and your listeners to stay on course.

4. Color the details but stay in the lines. It is nice when you take the audience on a journey and use beautiful literary language and descriptive words that take them into your story. It can be really captivating when you spend time coloring the details. I would say, however, don't make the illustration the focus. Remember you are illustrating a point, not illustrating an illustration. Also, if it is not in your personality to say things like "refreshing babbling brook cascading down a glistening rock", then I chill out, J.R.R. Tolkien, this is not for you.

The Anchor

An anchor is a sentence or a short paragraph proving that the truth, application, problem or illustration you are alluding to is connected to the Scriptures. In other words, it proves that your idea is *anchored* in the Scriptures.

One of the greatest compliments I have received and have given is telling someone that they stayed really close to the Scriptures the entire time. You can feel when a preacher is touching the Scriptures throughout their sermon. You can also feel when the Scripture is a sprinkle in or an afterthought. Since the word of God is alive and the power of your sermon, you will want to stay close to, and connected to, that power source. Anchoring through a short sentence can keep the preacher from wandering off track. It also helps your people learn by observation how to study the Bible. Hopefully, you are creating a culture where the sermon is a moment of corporate Scriptural study that serves as a launchpad for your listeners' week of intimacy with the Scriptures. It is critical that you include anchors throughout your process.

Redemptive Closure
Redemptive Closure is a sentence, paragraph or idea on how Jesus offers redemption to a specific problem you're addressing. Jesus is in the redemptive business. Jesus Christ is our redeemer! God created the world perfect and gave humans free will to enjoy the love and relationship of God on his own volition. The man and woman choose sin. That sin brings perversion and brokenness to everything on this planet. In steps Jesus! IN. STEPS. JESUS! Our Great Redeemer is plan A for redeeming all things. And, as we believers and preachers are priests ushering heaven down to earth and turning the faces of mankind upward in worship and surrender, it would behoove us to point out that everything has a redemptive ending if we would turn to Jesus. Every problem that we just pointed out in our sermon has a redeemer waiting to teach us what heaven looks like right now. That redeemer will eventually redeem all things for eternity as He creates a new heaven and new earth but pointing out that redemption now is a critical and core component for your sermon.

You can use Redemptive Closure to close out every sermon if you would like, or you can use it to close out a single truth! I had a mentor who would ask, "If you preach a sermon but don't get to the Gospel, did you really preach a sermon?" It is a fair question and what he meant by that was, did you show the love and power of our redeemer in your sermon? Did you tell the most important story of all time in your story? Because if we just present problems or big ideas without Jesus eventually redeeming it all, then we are just drawing people into religion and depression. If we just teach people how to put off the "old self" like Paul does in Ephesians 4, and we don't teach people how Jesus puts on the "new self", we have only told half the story.

Sermon with Core Components

Below, I have taken one of the connecting truths from our Mark 12 sermon and added what it looks like when application, anchor, illustration and redemptive closure are added. I will extract and expand on the connecting truth that performance is a bad motive.

Principal Truth--*When giving, Jesus cares more about the motive of your heart, than the measure in your hand.*
Principal Problem--*We tend to give from the motives of performance and religious reward rather than faith and worship.*
Principal Question--*What are the motives of your heart when you are giving to Jesus and His mission?*
Connecting Truths--*Good Motives*
1. Faith
2. Worship
Bad Motives
1. Performance
2. *Religious Reward*

Application- We have a big problem with performance in the church, don't we? I mean, Sunday morning is like a performance, and I am not talking about the preacher and worship team. We put on a religious performance for each other. It starts with a miserable car ride of tension. You're yelling at the kids and each other. You're bickering about not getting out of the house on time. But then we get to church, we get out of the car, and we wave with a big ole smile, "Hey brother, blessed in the Lord, praise the Lord. Hallelujah, amen. Selah." This is because we are conditioned to perform for each other. To put on masks and play a religious role. The main character in that role is perfect. We put on a perfect performance during worship, we know the accepted and safe positioning of the hands and the variations of a worship sway that will not be judged. We know how say hello and smile and wear the right clothing. If we know the passage that they are going to be in, we mark up our Bible to make people think we have read those Scriptures intently. Worse than all of this, we perform ourselves out of who we really are. If we are broken, we perform togetherness. If we are lost, we perform as one found and perfectly positioned. If we are addicted and ashamed, we perform as a saint who needs not the freedom of Christ. We perform ourselves away from living authentically with Jesus. We perform ourselves out of authentic community. We perform because we want Jesus to love us, and we want the

95

people to receive us. And giving is no different. Giving for many of us is an unhealthy performance masking guilt and hoping it will make people and Jesus love us. We need to bring death to religious performance.

Illustration- I remember the day my dad began to show me how to bring death to religious performance. I had been living this double life of performing in Church but having no real relationship with Jesus for over a decade. I thought that is what this whole thing was. I perform well and God rewards me. I perform well and church people accept me. Which, if you have forgotten, is every other religious paradigm out there. It's every other idea of God. I do this so you reward me. Right? That's what I thought this was. So, I was in the paper one Monday because the reporter had come to my church and was taking pictures because the church bought a school and moved in and was growing. And there I was, front page, praying over someone. I knew how to play the character. I knew how to play the role. I was a pastor's son! I was an expert! Well, the next week my fraudulent character was exposed. I was in the paper again for being the guy that somehow got two kegs at 17 years old, got a bunch of teens drunk and threw a party where another 16-year-old almost got beat to death. Not only was my performance exposed, but I exposed my dad's image. He was a pastor who could now lose this job at this big church. And I will never forget it. He called me into the kitchen. I thought I was done. I thought I was going to get a religious beat down. It was silent. Then my dad said to me. "Son, it's not going well right now, is it?" I said, "No, Dad". He said, "Can I hug you and pray for you?"

I was shocked. I expected religion and I got relationship. I expected a poor grade and I got intimacy and forgiveness. That's the day my dad taught me how to kill performance. How to look in my heart and ask, "Am I performing for a religious people and a religious figure or is my motive about faith, worship and a relationship with the Father who loves me?"

Anchor- See, Jesus kills performance here, doesn't He? There are two types of people in the room that Jesus is addressing. Those who perform really well; big robes, big money, big measure. And then the widow; no status, no stature, two pennies, poor performance. He calls His disciples to Him and says, "She wins!" She is giving not out of performance but of faith, devotion and a relationship with the Father. We must give like this woman. Not out of a performance-based religion. But out of a faith-filled, devoted relationship.

Redemptive Closure- Isn't this the Gospel? Our performance is filthy rags. Our performance means nothing to a Father who just wants our heart. He just wants our relationship. And the battle with this religious performance will go on and on. It will always be our tendency to perform for a Father who will love us regardless and just wants our intimacy. It is time to let God kill our performance and give from a place of faith, love and devotion.

Peripheral Practices

Remember, the core components that you just studied are meant to be the main focus. They are must haves. But you will also need to keep a circumferential and peripheral eye on these practices.

If your core components are the main organs in your body, these are the practices of the outsides that keep the insides healthy. If you keep a peripheral and consistent eye on these practices, the inside guts should be healthy.

Growing up, my family had this prayer that we would pray before dinner. It went, "Bless, O Lord, this food to our use and us to Thy service, amen." It's really simple, oddly beautiful and it is in my family heritage. The only issue is that we would often be sitting in front of a table of cholesterol and saturated fat. Because it was one of the prayers that we would say all the time, we would say it at McDonalds in front of a Big Mac with a Twinkie in our pockets. It seems like ironic temple stewardship to ask God to bless a Big Mac for my use and His service. I imagine God is up there wondering why He should somehow turn this burger into lettuce as it goes down my gullet. The practices that we adhere to on the outside will affect the inside organs. A lot of saturated fat and salt will harm your blood pressure and clog your arteries. A lot of alcohol will harm your liver. If you don't exercise with your body, your lungs and heart will simply not be healthy. If you don't adopt these peripheral practices, there is a good chance your inside core components will not be healthy, clear or have good flow. Here is the first one:

Inductive and Deductive Reasoning

Are you practicing a good balance of inductive and deductive reasoning?

Deductive reasoning is when you state a truth and then build from there. You proceed from the truth assertion and seek to prove it with examples, illustrations, and argumentation.

Inductive Reasoning is when you start with an illustration, story, or question and then build up to a truth. Deductive reasoning starts with an assertion of truth and then attempts to prove it. Inductive reasoning starts with an illustration or example of a truth then leads to the people to truth that lays behind the illustration.

Here is an example of how it would look using some core components.

Inductive Reasoning	Deductive Reasoning
Illustration	**Principal Truth**
Principal Problem	Principal Problem
Principal Question	Application
Principal Truth	Illustration
Connecting Truths	

You will notice on the left side of the diagram under Inductive Reasoning, there are components that use tension and mystery before the Principal Truth is stated. We will call these *tension components*. These main tension components are Illustration, Principal Problem and the Principal Question. All of these components don't answer the question, but provide problems and more questions.

On the right side of the diagram is a statement of the Principal Truth followed by a further breakdown of that truth. The Problem and the Illustration in that circumstance are shaped a little different because you have already given them the answer to the test.

Jesus and Paul used both in their preaching. Paul often used deductive reasoning in his letters. He would state a truth and then further explain what he meant by that truth or bring application to that truth.

"Children, obey your parents in the Lord, for this is right. "Honor your father and mother" (this is the first commandment with a promise), "that it may go well with you and that you may live long in the land." Fathers, do not provoke your children to anger, but bring them up in the discipline and instruction of the Lord." (Ephesians 6:1-4, ESV).

Paul states his claim about Godly family structure and then gives Scriptural support or an anchor, and then gives a connecting truth to family structure.

Jesus often taught inductively using components that provided a lot of tension and questions. I think the best example of this is in Jesus preaching of the Parable of the Sower in Matthew 13. He sits in a boat because of the crowds and tells them about a farmer sowing seed. He creates a bunch of tension in the crowd as He only describes the seed falling on four different surfaces and finding four different results and then he drops a bomb, "He who has ears let him hear". The disciples have a gut tornado from all of the tension and ask Jesus, "*Why do you speak to them in parables?*" (Matthew 13:10). Jesus had used Illustration to create tension, wonder and ownership of thought and question! He did it better than any of us will and then in one of the only moments He does this, He states the truth and explains the parable.

If you study the red letters in your Bible, you will find that Jesus mostly teaches inductively but absolutely teaches deductively at times in what we have recorded. You will lead one way or the other. The point is, as a peripheral practice, make sure you try and balance it out quite a bit.

You are telling a story, not teaching a seminary class. A seminary class, at least the classes I took, were mostly statements and explanations to follow. A whole lot of deductive teaching, as the professor aimed to cover a lot of material in an hour. You are, however, telling a story with arc and mystery. You are creating questions and helping to answer them. You are doing deep deductive dives into important theological topics, and you are doing it in a majority monologue setting not a majority dialogue setting.

Repetitive String

Do you have careful and intentional repetition strung throughout your message?

If you are reading this with someone or near someone, do me a favor and give them a stern and confident look and repeat this phrase to them, "Repetition is good." We are all tempted to be clever and unique, and the thought of using repetition seems stale and tired—this couldn't be more wrong.

We have all heard preachers lament that no one remembers what they say. Too often, they don't even remember what they say. We have also heard the listener mourn that they didn't know exactly what the preacher was trying to say. Some of that is the problem we have been contending with all along. The problem that being faithful to clarity is a difficult endeavor. But the other reason for the lack of clarity and recall is that we don't value careful and intentional repetition. A good peripheral practice is to figure out which core components you want people to take home with them, and then repeat them. Repeat them at multiple junctures throughout your sermon. String the same sentence in and out, weaving it into your sermon until the very end.

5 ways to use Repetition or Repetitive String

1. *Use it to make your illustration more powerful-* At times your story will wander, or your illustration will meander off of its intended path. Shrinking what you want to say down to a concise and compelling sentence will not only help you with clarity but repeating it three or four times throughout your illustration will cement that idea in your listeners mind and remind them why you went into that illustration in the first place.

2. *Use it to tie your idea or application back to your core component-* We have stated in this process that most components and ideas should be connected to your Principal Truth. We have even named "connecting truths" what we have named them, so there is no confusion on if they need to be connected or not. One of the best and easiest ways to do this is repetition.

3. *Use it to land the plane-* It is perfectly acceptable to conclude your sermon by repeating your most important components. Not only will it alert people that the landing gear is out, but it will remind people what they should take home with them.

4. *Use it when what you just said was really good-* Does that sound bad? The truth is you have done a lot of work crafting some sentences and ideas. Something will either be really anointed or really tweetable. It is ok to say that again and say it slowly with some emphasis.

5. *Use it when you have lost your place-* We have all wandered away from our manuscript or outline that is located on the pulpit or table. That dreaded moment where you feel a bit naked in front of a bunch of people because you forgot what comes next. The best thing is to slowly repeat what you just said. Slowly….repeat…what…you…just…said…while…you make your way back…to….the….po-d-i-um.

Contextual Texture

Do you have relevant contextual texture and coloring in the lines of your Principal Truth, Principal Problem, Connecting Truths and/or Application?

The compelling Scriptural narratives and the colorful context that lies in them are downright fascinating. Once you start to learn all the feels and textures of historical context, you can't help but join the nerd club. The 66 books written over centuries in bustling cities, thriving seaports, prisons and house arrest contain nerd-nugget gold. Give me a nerd patch now, and I will sow it onto my nerd vest. However, it is important that you locate and leverage the relevant Contextual Texture; remember that all of what you learned and are intrigued by is not relevant to the application or truth you are trying to communicate. Let's define contextual texture by breaking it up and then talk about where and how it is best used.

Context- a simple Google search will tell you that context is, *the circumstances that form the setting for an event, statement, or idea, and in terms of which it can be fully understood and assessed.* In other words, you did all this research in your exegetical endeavors, and you learned the context of the text.

Texture- *the feel, appearance, or consistency of a surface or substance.* Good texture describes the feel and appearance so well, you could have a blindfold on and still know the essence of that thing or place. For example, the way the texture of a certain blanket brings you to a comfortable and familiar location or the way a good description of fear in a novel brings your own emotions to that place. You coloring in the contextual lines of your text will be critical to the depth into the text you are able to take your listener.

Let's put it all together.

Contextual Texture- Describing relevant historical and cultural nuances in a way that will help your people feel the place and time the author is communicating from and therefore help your audience better understand the truth that author is communicating.

Because the possibilities are endless but the preacher's time is not, we should focus on how to find and leverage the most relevant contextual texture. Every preacher will express a different level of interest. Meaning some of you will absolutely enjoy finding every nook and cranny that makes up the context of the text. Some will not have the same level of interest vigor. There will also be a great scale of time. Some preachers will designate four hours for sermon prep and some will designate 15, depending on the value placed on preaching and/or the place that preaching fits inside the vision and mission of the church. Because the scale is so high, low, narrow and wide, the goal of this section will be to give you a flexible framework that can be sensitive to every preacher. This flexible framework should help:

Document during exegetical research- Hopefully, you didn't rush your exegetical process. Better yet, hopefully you really took your time in the exegetical section. This is one of the greatest joys of preaching. You are drinking in deep the Scriptures and their meaning for your life and those to whom you will boldly proclaim your findings. Therefore, it is a great practice to write down, mark up, question and find answer to what you are studying when it comes to context. However you best take notes, and this will vary also, write down everything interesting you are leaning about context. This will give you great reference material when you are crafting your sermon. The truth is, you may only use 10% of it in your sermon, but 100% will be valuable to your relationship with Jesus and His Scriptures in the end.

Utilize good sources and don't overcommit- The age of information is trying to suck you into a mass disinformation tornado. Everyone is a genius, and we have a significant source that rhymes with Trikipedia where anyone can contribute to absolute truth. Make sure your source is trusted. Arrive at their website or to their commentary with a bit of skepticism and a whole lot of Holy Spirit discernment. And when you get to the message, you also don't need to overcommit. Meaning, you can always preface a comment with a notion that this is not absolute truth, and you are making a few assumptions when it comes to that particular contextual note.

Color and Shade- Feeding bland information without attempting to add feeling, emotion and colorful detail will make this practice weak. In the same way you tell story with coloring in the lines and shading boundaries, color and shade the details of history and context. Take your listener to Sodom and Gomorrah and help them feel how far that land was from God. Take them to the unknown of the wilderness and the hunger of the prophet.

Keep your gate narrow- Remember the Gate Principle. It is easier to keep something out than kick something out. You will discover a lot of riveting biblical information. You will be tempted to build a sermon off of a sub point that has little to do with the heart of what the author is saying. Document this information for later use when crafting your sermon and make sure that it is absolutely relevant to your truth, application or problem.

Discussion and Practice

1. What is your go-to sermon structure? Which structure from the structures listed are you most comfortable with?

___

2. Which principle out of the three principles (Gate, Shrink, and Hermeneutics for Culture) do you struggle with the most? How can you improve?

___

Take one Scripture and build out a simple outline using these Core Components. If you shrink these components down to a few sentences, it will help you work on being concise in your preaching.

Principal Truth

___

Principal Problem

___

Principal Question

___

Connecting Truth 1

___

Anchor:

_____

_____

Illustration:

_____

_____

_____

_____

_____

Application:

_____

_____

_____

Connecting Truth 2

_____

_____

_____

Anchor:

_____

_____

Illustration:

_____

_____

_____

_____

_____

Application:

_____

_____

_____

Redemptive Closure:

_____

_____

_____

PART 3 THE PREACHER'S DELIVERY

CHAPTER 7

GET OUT OF THE WAY

Getting yourself out of the way, but being yourself all the way

In one of the most purchased and peddled Christian books of all time, *"A Purpose Driven Life"*[15], Rick Warren dropped this dime on us all: "It's not about you". As a young man who was just entering a life with Christ, this was a profound revelation. I just spent 17 years thinking that I was the axis that the world revolved around. Now I need to focus my mind and heart on Christ and others. In my denomination, the Christian and Missionary Alliance, we talk about sanctification being both positional and progressive. We are sanctified in Christ positionally. Yet we are also on a long, slow and winding road toward Christlikeness. The discovery that the world does not revolve around me fits in the latter category; it's an arduous path toward sacrifice in Christ. I don't think I am going too far out on a limb when I assume we all struggle to walk this long and winding road of surrender.

Most new and young preachers I have encountered struggle deeply with being in their own head. They are engaging all sorts of "what ifs" and doubts that plague them. They are thinking about all of their own flaws and sins. Like Moses, they come to God with a litany of reasons why they are not the ones to deliver the powerful news. Maybe they are thinking along the same lines as Moses, and they are not confident in the fluidity of their speech. Maybe they are thinking about a persistent sin that, in their mind, somehow disqualifies them from the moment of standing up in front of others to share God's word. Maybe they are thinking about the people in the audience the way Moses did. In the same way he was concerned with the opinion of one of the most powerful leaders in all the land, they are concerned about the opinionated elder in the second row.

It was a debilitating moment for Moses, wasn't it? Even though the

---

[15] Warren, R. *A Purpose Driven Life*. Published by Zondervan, Grand Rapids, MI, 2002, pp 17.

God of his forefathers chose to speak to him out of a bush that was on fire but somehow not being consumed. Even though God was cluing him in to His compassion and plan, Moses was debilitated. The conversation went on a lot longer than God was comfortable with. I have often felt that way; unworthy and unqualified. Unworthy. Unqualified. It is debilitating. Maybe you feel this way as well. You have listed all the reasons why you are the wrong person to stand before God's people and preach his word. The laundry list is long and the time is short. The reckoning is coming in under 24 hours and you are having anxiety dreams about standing up in front of people and forgetting your notes. Side note: we have all had those, you are not weird.

It's in this vacillating storm of thought that you must hear how God responds to Moses. As He comforts and, at times, rebukes Moses, He speaks to the preacher's soul. First God says, *"But I will be with you, and this shall be the sign for you, that I have sent you: when you have brought the people out of Egypt, you shall serve God on this mountain"* (Exodus 3:12, ESV). The words, "But I will be with you" will be said to Gideon, Joshua, Abraham, the Disciples and many other soon-to-be mavericks throughout the Scriptures. God is trying to turn their eyes from their own weaknesses and readjust their attention to His strength. We often need to take our eyes off our smallness in order to see His bigness. Only then are we ready to step into the moment. The proximity of God should bring a wave of confidence and comfort over us that helps us move differently into the pulpit. Moses, however, will need more convincing.

"Then Moses said to God, 'If I come to the people of Israel and say to them, 'The God of your fathers has sent me to you,' and they ask me, 'What is his name?' what shall I say to them?' God said to Moses, 'I AM WHO I AM.' And he said, 'Say this to the people of Israel: 'I AM has sent me to you''" (Exodus 3:13-14, ESV).

In this passage, God issues the greatest mic-drop of all time when he says, "I am the essence and meaning of all that is good and powerful." In other words, "I am the answer to every pressing and foundational question you have". Who is all powerful? I AM. Who is the future of your people? I AM. Who is the comfort for your anxiety and worry? I AM. All of the questions that Moses has in this moment are answered in the identity of the God who has just promised His proximity, presence and power. Even after all of this, Moses— just like many of us— still needs convincing

After Moses receives some signs and wonders including a leprous hand that is healed in an instant and a staff that turns into a serpent and then back into a staff again, he still cries out in a petulant manner, "*Oh, my Lord, I am not eloquent, either in the past or since you have spoken to your servant, but I am slow of speech and of tongue*" (Exodus 4:10, ESV). It is Moses' last attempt to convince God that He has called the wrong guy. We have all been there. We have all made our self the center of the world before preaching. May I remind you of the times you listed off your sin to God or listed off your weaknesses as if you were giving God some sort of amazing revelation. As if God is up there thinking, "O yea, you know what? You are right, let me choose someone else for this." As Moses proclaims the weakness of his speech, an excuse I am not sure he really has, having grown up in a palace and having a tremendous education, God will respond in what seems to be a moment of frustration: "*Then the Lord said to him, 'Who has made man's mouth? Who makes him mute, or deaf, or seeing, or blind? Is it not I, the Lord? Now therefore go, and I will be with your mouth and teach you what you shall speak.*" (Exodus 4:11-12, ESV).

"*Who made man's mouth?*" God has had it. He shouldn't have had to wield this revelation weapon over Moses. He shouldn't have to remind Moses that his lack of confidence was in a gift God had given him. Does that sink in for you?

In other words, get yourself out of the way. Get out of your head. This is not about you; this moment is about God. He asked you to be faithful and being faithful doesn't mean listing off all the reasons you are unqualified. It means listing off the reasons why God is qualified. I often ask new preachers three questions: 1. Is God's Word alive? 2. Does God want to speak to His people? 3. Does God use unworthy and unqualified people throughout the Scriptures? And if you answered those questions the way that all the others have… you can march into enemy territory and proclaim God's message with power. The truth is, you will probably have to preach a message to yourself before you preach a message to others. God is calling you to proclaim His truth boldly and He is very capable of using any conduit or tool that He chooses.

Maybe the last section did not minister to you in a way that you needed. Maybe you don't really struggle with a lack of confidence in gifting or communication. However, you struggle with sin. It is shocking to you that you sinned Friday night and somehow, in your naked and ashamed state, you need to stand up in front of people and proclaim truth on Sunday morning. Often, preachers will ask if they should even walk up to that pulpit after sinning. Moses' questions were not just about his gifting qualification, they were also about his purity qualifications. He had murdered a guy, so he had a decent reason. But, in similar fashion, this wasn't about Moses. Moses' leadership ability and purity didn't qualify him, God qualified him. The fundamental flaw in your lack of confidence of self is you are forgetting that you didn't die for your own sin. Your righteousness didn't come from your works, it comes from grace, and therefore you don't qualify yourself to speak in front of people. A loving Savior who died for you, in spite of all of your gross mess, qualifies you.

So, get out of the way. Make room for Jesus. It is not about you; it is all about Him. Walk up to that pulpit with confidence. Not confidence in yourself but in God, His word, and the truth that God wants to accomplish his purposes through you—not because of who you are, but because of who He is.

The Other Side

The Spirit often reminds me, as I go in and out of all sorts of preaching environments, "Don't be too big or too small for any environment or situation". For some of you, getting out of the way doesn't mean finding confidence in God and getting over the anxiety of self. For some, it's about pride, not fear. For you it is the other side of the coin… you tend to be too big for an environment. It is still about you, your gifting and your ability. I can't think of a quicker way to bomb a sermon. It is always the sermons that I go into thinking, "Ugh, this crowd is small," or "Wow, I really have a good product here," that will undoubtedly be a pulpit pipe bomb. Yes, I do think those fleshly things; yes, I am ashamed of them, and yes, it is really poor theology. Hopefully, my vulnerability has helped drive confession for you, and you will admit that, at times, you are too big for the moment, and you need to take that to Jesus. While praying, "Jesus will you humble me?" might be the most dangerous prayer on the planet, it is also one of the most critical prayers a preacher can pray.

It is critical to test the other side. It is important to go into the pulpit with the correct heart and perspective. Not necessarily for the product of preaching, but for the process of the preacher. This is just as much about God ministering to your heart as it is His ministry to the people that will hear it. If God is going to transform the hearts and minds of the people through this preaching experience it is not because of you, but it involves you and includes you.

Discussion and Practice

1. List 3 ways you have gotten in the way of what God wants to deliver in the pulpit.

i._____

_____

_____

ii._____

_____

_____

iii._____

_____

_____

2. How have you been either too big or too small for the environments you are preaching in?

_____

_____

_____

_____

_____

_____

CHAPTER 8

ANOINTED PREACHING VS. ANEMIC PREACHING

Anemic Preaching

Anemia: a condition marked by a deficiency of red blood cells or of hemoglobin in the blood, resulting in pallor and weariness.

We have all sat under anemic preaching. It lacks blood flow, power and comes off as pale. There is no punch, and you leave the sanctuary or the home feeling like you didn't go to meet with God and His Word, but you met with someone's anemic monologue. We have addressed Anemic preaching in Chapter 5 and have stated one of the major reasons for the lack of power. If the Scriptures are not the source of your Principal Truth or the heartbeat of your sermon, there will be no blood flow.

However, there are other reasons for anemic preaching. I have sat under preachers where I have read their manuscripts and, previous to their sermon, there was evidence of a good manuscript with good technique and tactic. The approach was compelling, and the structure was clear. The delivery had cadence and performance, and yet anemia marked the moment. That's because there are plenty of contributors to the disease of anemic preaching.

For instance, public enemy number one is typically the preacher (see Chapter 8). But it may also be that the people do not have the right soil of heart to plant seeds among. Preaching should be dialogue, not monologue. We are all coming to the table of God, hungry together and participating in the proclamation of the Word of God. Sometimes, the people are anemic and there is no agreement with the power in the room. There is no hunger and humility and that contributes to the atmosphere of preaching. There could be corporate sin clogging the ears and eyes of the people. There could be a Pharisee culture or a Spirit of defiance to the Word of God. There are many contributing factors to anemic preaching, but the easy target is a lack of anointing.

Anointed Preaching

Anointing can be an elusive idea throughout the Scriptures. Especially as anointing is deeply associated with the Spirit of God. Jesus gives this nugget to Nicodemus; *"The wind blows where it wishes, and you hear it's sound, but you do not know where it comes from or where it goes. So it is with everyone who is born of the Spirit."* (John 3:8, ESV). Now, this is clearly a conversation about being born again and born of the Spirit, but the characterization of who the Spirit is and the renegade nature in which the Holy Spirit moves still stand. This Scripture reminds us that the Spirit will not be controlled by a religious order or a works-based recipe. God is God; He touches, He anoints, He is the Sovereign One.

Anointing originates with sheep and shepherds, which is highly appropriate and strategic by God. Insects would get into the wool of sheep and eventually the nose or ears. These insects became deadly and would consume the brain and kill the sheep. In order to protect the sheep, the shepherd would pour oil over the sheep's head to protect it.

This practice throughout the Old Testament meant that a person, when anointed, was protected and empowered by the Great Shepherd. This King or Prophet has been touched by God. God sees them, He covers them, and if they will follow the Shepherd, they will be used for His service.

The New Testament understanding of anointing follows suit, as it is associated with the touch of God through the Holy Spirit. The Greek word for anoint is *Chrio* which means "to smear or rub with oil". God does ask us to anoint the sick in James 5, but the narrative of anointing throughout the Scriptures is that it is a touch from God, and there is a choosing from God that goes along with it.

Anointing is a lot like a shooting star; you know it when you see it, it's amazing, and it's hard to predict or prepare for. You walk out of a sermon and tell your friend, "Man, that person was anointed" or "that worship was anointed." That's because you felt the touch of God in the room. God chose that person in that moment in that place and moved through them to touch others. There is an everlasting joy in the room. The truth is raw and untainted by excuse. Following this touch of God is salvation, baptism and life change. This is why we do what we do; to see heaven collide with earth and, for that moment, to turn into intimacy and submission. And although we will never control the Spirit of God, I do believe we can faithfully position ourselves to be conduits of his love.

113

Faithfully Positioning Ourselves

Embrace a Pneumatology- You will have high, gaudy blockades up against a move of God if you don't embrace a faithful Pneumatology. Pneumatology means "study of the Spirit" and some folks still view the Holy Spirit as an optional inclusion to the Trinity; a Person they may shut out as their theological background or level of comfort dictate. Maybe it is the Church you grew up in, or the historical denomination you are immersed in, but you have no thoughtful view of the Holy Spirit. Or you have embraced a heretical view that has led you to build walls so high that God needs to send a catapult to break into your fortress. That is not faithful positioning. It is critical for you to take action to remedy this positional issue. 1. Read some books on the person of the Holy Spirit. 2. Interact with your charismatic brothers and sisters and study their pneumatology with an open heart. 3. Confess that your new trinity of the Father the Son and the Holy Bible is not the true Trinity and admit that this new pneumatology is actually an old heresy. 4. Do a personal and comprehensive study on what Jesus says about the Holy Spirit. 5. Surrender to the whole of the Trinity and embrace the beauty and wonder of the Holy Spirit. That is faithful positioning.

*Care about the life behind the pulpit-*Another way to faithfully position yourself is to understand that your private life is much more important than your public life. The gifting that you reveal above the surface is much less critical than the heart you foster below the surface. Jesus is quite firm here, isn't He? *"I am the vine; you are the branches. Whoever abides in me and I in them, will produce much fruit, for apart from me you can do nothing"* (John 15:5, ESV). Apart from Me you can do nothing! If you do not have a deep, abiding relationship with God, you will not have an anointed preaching life. You may perform well and produce a decent "talk", but you will not position yourself faithfully for anointing. This also goes with whatever Scripture you are speaking on that day as well. If you don't let that Scripture impact your private life—if you don't let it speak to your heart—you will not discover the implications for yourself. It is hard to have an authentic conversation with your people if you have not allowed the Holy Spirit to first speak to you from the Scripture you are preaching.

Pray with a heart of submission and a goal of saturation- It is faithful positioning to recognize that you are the under-shepherd. You don't have the ability to anoint and choose yourself. You cannot manufacture your spiritual gift. It is just that…a gift. You should have a posture of submission when walking up to the pulpit to preach. Know that the Anointed One has all the power and longs to give it to His child, but if His child has a heart of entitlement or pride, the Spirit of God stands in opposition. If you need a heart of submission to faithfully position yourself, you also need a goal of saturation. Prayer should saturate your entire process from before you approach and study the text until you finish preaching that text. This will facilitate your heart of submission. My denomination stands on this principle, "Prayer is the primary work of God's people." What that statement ultimately means is that God is everything. He is "I AM". He goes before all, is in all, and all that we do is in worship of Him. Therefore, prayer needs to be as Corrie Ten Boom states "The steering wheel" not the "spare tire".

Discussion and Practice

1. What did you learn about anointing that can help your preaching?

_____

_____

_____

_____

_____

_____

2. How can you better position yourself to be filled with/walk with the Holy Spirit?

_____

_____

_____

_____

_____

_____

3. What part does prayer play in your preaching process currently? How can prayer and listening take a bigger role in your preaching?

_____

_____

_____

_____

_____

_____

CHAPTER 9
INTERNALIZATION AND DELIVERY

You have a mostly finished product in front of you. There will be tweaks and changes as you internalize. Every once in a while, God will ask you to just throw the whole thing out and preach something different. That's…fun. Let's pretend this is not that moment, though. You went through good process from prayer to exegesis while applying good hermeneutic, to more prayer, to wrestling with the Scriptural proclamations in your own heart, to building and crafting a sermon faithful to both the text and to clarity. Now what?

Well, you have to take it from the paper (digital or otherwise) to your innards. The concepts, wording, Principal Truth and Connecting Truths need to connect to the deepest places of you. Just memorizing something won't work. You should feel the truth and mean what you say because of the depth of ownership you have. As Jewish thought goes, it should be in your heart, the central seat of your thoughts. It should make the long two-foot journey from head to heart and then back out of your mouth as it picks up momentous passion and emotion along the way. This is internalization.

Practicing Good Internalization

This is where a lot of preachers get tripped up. They feel like they have done the work. They let their minds rest and their bodies slump as if they have crossed the finish line. The finish line comes much later, and if you don't decide to have a good internalization process, there is a good chance you will stand behind the pulpit and not connect with your audience. There is nothing worse than Captain Staresatnotes, so don't be one. Resolve today to be a preacher that doesn't just create a sermon and read it. Resolve to preach the Word of God from your guts, as if it is a part of who you are. You are holding onto it like a hot potato, and you have to give it to someone else. You are pregnant with what God has been teaching you and it is time to give birth. The essence of internalization is in the definition.

Internalization- make [attitudes or behavior] part of one's nature by learning or unconscious assimilation.

In this case, you will want to make your sermon a part of your nature. I know that this may seem like a daunting task as those words sink in. But fret not, you will get better at this as time goes on. Unfortunately, I smoked a lot of pot before I knew Jesus, so my muscle grew quite a bit slower, but your short-term memory operates like a muscle in that it will grow stronger with use. That is… science… I think.

Where to Start

In the same way that order mattered in your crafting phase, it matters in your internalization phase. You will need to develop an internalization process that works for you. It will change and take new shape as you discover what works better for your rhythm and ministry life. My process used to look like this:

Read manuscript three times on Wednesday.
Read manuscript three times on Thursday.
Give my brain a break on Friday (Sabbath).
Preach while slowly disconnecting from notes on Saturday morning.
Preach while slowly disconnecting further from notes on Saturday night.
Preach it Sunday morning before the service until I need to reference my notes very little.

One Saturday, I was out to dinner with my wife and another couple. I couldn't help but open the needy mental folder of internalizing my sermon over and over again. All I could think about is, "I gotta get home." I realized, right there, that I did this all the time on Saturdays. I was connected to my manuscript all day even though it wasn't in front of me. It wasn't fair to me or my family, and it didn't make me a better preacher. It made me an "I lose every Saturday" bitter preacher. As Lecrae says in one of his songs[16], "*They say don't get bitter, get better, I am working on switching those letters*". I decided to make a change. I would, from now on, wake up early on Saturday mornings and do the two runs through my sermon early in the morning. That worked out better; the content was fresh and knowing that the rest of the day was dedicated to my family was worth it.

You will find your rhythm. It will take some time and giving yourself the freedom to adjust, tweak and grow. Now would be a good time to start to develop that rhythm. Write out a schedule and stick to it for a few months. Practice your craft over and over until it becomes second nature and part of you. It will be best if you start to view that time as an intimate time with Jesus. He gave you that truth, and you are trying to learn it deeply while sharing with Him your feelings, hopes and aspirations for this message going out.

---

[16] Lecrae, *I'll Find You* ft. Tori Kelly. Track 11 on All Things Work Together, produced by Danny Majic & DJ Frank E, 2017.

Hopefully, you have caught that this process is like a garden walk with Jesus. You and Him, all of who you are, breathing out honesty and your love for the Text and His people.

As you find a rhythm, it will help you find unction to persevere through this process if you think of internalization as *closing the distance*. That is really what internalization helps you do. When you get up in front of the people, there will be a human distance between you and them. They have baggage and so do you. They don't know what you have been through with this Scripture, and they don't know what you have been through as a human in relationship with God this week. The same goes for you in reference to them. You will have a few stories at that time, but the gap is still wide. If you stand behind a big pulpit and a big manuscript, you will not close the distance. That pulpit and manuscript can easily turn into a wall. You owning that Scripture and the truth that God gave you, where it has become a part of your nature, will close that gap. You will connect with them because you are not gripping onto a piece of paper. You are expressing the grace and the natural outflow of what lives inside of you.

The Internalization Big 5

1. *Surrender this process once again to Jesus!* This time of internalization is a time of intimacy. Ask the Good Teacher to teach you more. Ask Him to grow you and be present as you soak in what He has given you.

2. *Read and Repeat.* The easiest way to begin an internalization process is to read it over and over again. I read my whole manuscript about six times before I start to feel like I have the ideas and big moments memorized enough where I can disconnect from it.

3. *Begin to Rehearse.* Your rehearsal can look however you want it to. Some of you will need to process this out loud, or in front of a mirror. I, personally, at the very least need to whisper it. I love to have a quiet space somewhere where no one will hear me and think I am a weirdo. Now is the time to start to take your eyes off the page a bit and preach it out loud.

4. *Rinse and Repeat.* Continue to rehearse, read and rehearse again until that Word is in your soul! I feel good about my internalization when I only really need to look at each page once. I have a six-page manuscript and so that is a hopeful six times total.

5. *Establish and Tweak Rhythm.* What worked for you and what didn't? It is a

moving target, internalization, and that is ok.

The Moment

The preacher sometimes shakes as he or she is finally making their way to the pulpit. It all culminates and rests here. This moment feels different for every preacher, but most preachers are fully dependent and vulnerable in this moment. If God doesn't show up and this is just a demonstration of self or a cleverly crafted monologue, it was all for naught. But if God would step into that pulpit with you and if you will deliver the message remembering that God longs to speak, He longs to teach His people, and He longs to bring His story alive out of the only living book we have on this planet, then something special may just happen. I am glad you made it here. Don't live in fear. Embrace this moment with your Father. He loves you and is fully present.

Delivery Notes

Delivery is critical for 95% of the preachers I listen to. I listen to a wide-ranging gambit of preachers, and only a few of them don't need a compelling delivery system. It seems like Tim Keller knows how good his content is. Bill Johnson delivers a soft pillow cadence and somehow keeps me from sleeping with his unique thought and compelling one-liners. Delivery will most likely be critical for you because you are neither of those people. Because of that, I would like to close this out with some real practical notes on delivery. I gave you a "Big 5" for internalization and so let's stick with a Big 5 for delivery.

The Delivery Big 5

1. *Connect with Jesus.* If you can't tell, one of my favorite things about being a preacher is it brings me closer to Him and His Word. It may even feel like cheating sometimes, because I always have a message I am bringing to His feet and other people don't get that privilege. I don't care if it is cheating, I want to be close to Jesus. The moment is coming and therefore your desperation level is high. This is a good thing, and it will drive you to your knees. Pray a lot before each message.

2. *Be You.* One more time for the folks in the nose bleeds. This is not time to impersonate your favorite preacher or try to be someone you are not. The people that know me know that my volume hits really high levels when I am talking about cereal, so they know it is still me when I am hitting even higher

volumes about Jesus. If you are a quiet thoughtful communicator in life, that might be your natural mode in the pulpit. That is ok, and there are some really effective quiet and thoughtful communicators. If people smell the inauthentic, they begin to check out or lose trust. If people sense performance and acting, they will choose to treat the truth that you are communicating as cheap and consumeristic. It is critical that you be yourself in this moment. However, I must note that you are talking about the word of God! So, no matter how collected and reserved you are in real life, they must see the passion in whatever volume you use. They must feel your love for Jesus and the text in that moment, whether you are a loud, quiet, or heart monitor preacher. Sometimes, I will leave a sermon and think, "That preacher might as well have been talking about different types of top-soil". They lacked conviction and passion, and I felt like Jesus had not resurrected from the dead yet, their delivery was so lacking. The point is, conviction and passion come in many different forms, and you will need to resolve to embody the personality God gave you, lit on fire by the passion and Spirit of God.

3. *Pray for the room.* It always connects me to the Father's heart for His people when I pray for the room. If I get a chance to listen to a worship team's practice or walk around each chair and pray for the people, it brings the message into perspective. I am delivering light to many people living in darkness. It is a sobering and helpful thought. It also puts my narcissism in check. Preaching can be a narcissistic exercise. We can easily become self-consumed and tell stories about ourselves and think about ourselves while maybe even being on a big screen. Then, afterward, we will think about the feedback that we will get or the people we may have pleased. All of that feedback needs to roll off the back like water off a duck, but even that exercise can be a self-consuming one. Praying for the room can help you focus on the fact that Jesus wants to meet with people today. He wants to heal their deepest and darkest, He wants to give them hope, and He wants to transform lives.

4. *Cadence is Critical.* Although the needle will move at a different meter for every preacher, cadence will still be critical. There will need to be some up and down. Some thoughtful, slow and repetitive as well as some pressing and unctuous proclamation. Your cadence should go up and down because the story does. There will be a climax in the Principal Truth, a real bummer in the Principal Problem and some real intrigue in the context. Because of that, let your cadence go with the story. Every song has a cadence, every story has a cadence and so will every sermon.

Your cadence will be best when it is natural, when the ups and downs mean something to you, and you have decided to let the people see how much they

121

mean. As you draw yourself or let God draw you out from behind the pulpit, your body language and mannerisms show the people exactly how much hurt or joy that brings you. Your cadence will also be best when you are not rushing or panicking. For the first 500 sermons or so, I had to continuously tell myself to slow down. I had to ask God before every sermon to give me the right pace. Usually, during that sermon, He would show me that either I lacked confidence in the content or what He was doing and that is why I was moving so fast. Your pace will say a lot about your process. But make no mistake, cadence and pace are critical. Pay attention to them and take care of that element of your delivery.

5. *Once it is over, put it away.* I know this may not seem like it fits seamlessly into the delivery category. But I am parting ways with you for now and wanted to give a parting thought. If you are going to run a marathon of preaching week and week out, you will need to be ok with being faithful. You were faithful this week to the Scriptures, to your God and to your people. You may have stuttered a few times or accidentally cussed, thinking it meant something different (that happened to me). The point is that your next sermon is coming soon, and a perfect sermon cannot be your goal. Being faithful to Jesus and loving your people have to be your goals. So, take a few notes on what you can do better next time and then sleep well at night.

I hope and pray that this journey is a joy to you. I hope you find Jesus in a deeper way and teach others to do the same. I leave you with the words of God spoken to Joshua as he took up an impossible mantle. "Be strong and courageous."

Discussion and Practice

1. Now that you have gone through the book, how has your weekly process changed since Chapter 3? Write it out again

Monday-

Tuesday-

Wednesday-

Thursday-

Friday-

Saturday-

Sunday-

2. What are some helpful additions to your process?

_____
_____
_____
_____
_____
_____

3. Did you meet some of the goals you set out to meet when you started this book? If so, which ones?

_____
_____
_____
_____
_____
_____

4. In Chapter 9, you were given an "Internalization Big 5". After reading this book, what are your Preaching Big 5? In other words, what are the top 5 elements you will add to your preaching process today?

1.

2.

3.

4.

5

Made in the USA
Monee, IL
30 January 2022

90217656R00072